BURGUNDIANS IN THE MIST

BY

MARC A. COMTOIS

Marc A. Comtois

DEDICATION

To my wife for her love, understanding and patience.
Without her, I never could have traveled this path.

To my daughters, Abigail and Mary, for always asking
questions and making me think.

To my parents for their constant support.

To Jeanne Comtois, Mémère, for giving me the gift of
reading over so many years.

Marc A. Comtois

CONTENTS

ACKNOWLEDGMENTS

First and foremost, I'd like to thank Dr. Donna T. McCaffrey of Providence College for her guidance, particularly in medieval matters, but also those both historiographical and methodical. It takes a rare person to make the latter interesting! I'd also like to thank those who have guided me through history over the years, particularly my High School History teacher (and soccer coach!) Mr. Stuart Durrell; Dr. Robert Gardella and Dr. Jacques Szaluta of the U.S. Merchant Marine Academy; and Dr. Thomas W. Grzebien III, Dr. Robert McCarthy and Dr. Richard Grace of Providence College.

Marc A. Comtois

Author's Note

   Burgundians in the Mist is based on a Masters Thesis delivered in 2006 at Providence College. My goal was to write a historical narrative accessible to the general reader but with footnotes provided for specialists.   As I've studied history, I've come to value scholarship that utilizes the footnote to provide the reader with a secondary, historiographical work that runs below the main narrative. I've attempted to follow that model.

   Regarding terminology, traditional classifications--such as using "tribes" to identify a group of "barbarians"--have given way to softer terms like "peoples" or "groups." Thus, one scholar's "Germanic People" is another's "Barbarian Tribe." I use these various terms interchangeably. Then there are the names. Nearly every German seems to have at least 3 variations (ie; Clothilde, Chrotochildis, Clotilda, etc.). I have picked one and attempted to be consistent throughout.

   Since I initially completed this work, books by Peter Heather (*The Fall of the Roman Empire: A New History of Rome and the Barbarians*) and Brian Ward-Perkins (*The Fall of Rome and the End of Civilization*), among others, have added significantly to the study of this period. Unfortunately, with one exception, these and other works published after 2006 are not cited herein because, at some point, one simply has to stop researching and get the thing published! The exception is *The Legend of Sigurd and Gudrún* by J.R.R. Tolkien (edited by his son Christopher), which was released in 2009. I used it to supplement and update Chapter 4 (dealing with Burgundians in myth and legend). Now, into the mist.

Marc Comtois
23 May 2011

Marc A. Comtois

INTRODUCTION

"Who Are Those Guys?"

The above quote from the movie *Butch Cassidy and the Sundance Kid* came to mind when I first started reading about the Burgundians. Because the Burgundians have left very few written documents, their historical legacy has more often been described and defined by others. The story of the Burgundians has usually been interspersed throughout more generalized accounts of the Germanic migrations or the fall of the Western Roman Empire. Most often, the Burgundians of the fifth and sixth centuries have been portrayed as bit players in the history of the Merovingian Franks, particularly by Merovingian partisans such as Gregory of Tours. Few narratives have described the nature and evolution of particular aspects of Burgundian society throughout history.

What do we know? We know that the Burgundians were a Germanic tribe who crossed the Rhine and settled in Roman Gaul in the fifth century. Historians have traditionally traced their origins to Scandinavia and to tribes mentioned in various ancient Greek and Roman accounts. Modern historians have questioned these classical sources and assert that the true origin of the Burgundians, as of many Germanic tribes, remain hidden in the mist of time. Some claim that a history of the Burgundians could only properly start in the fourth century, when they are clearly first referred to by the 4th century Roman historian Ammianus Marcellinus.

The Burgundians who crossed the Rhine in A.D. 406 were not an ethnically homogenous sub-set of Germans, but rather a group of Germans, some probably with Roman blood, who were united by shared traditions and strong leaders. Like the other Germanic kingdoms, that of the Burgundians was an "elaborate synthesis of various elements, and the creation of a new civilization distinct both from that of late Antiquity and from that of Free Germany. It can be judged inferior to classical civilization, but its originality cannot be denied, and it cannot be considered simply as an indefinitely prolonged period of 'decadence.'"[1]

Thus, the Burgundians of the fifth and sixth centuries may have been only tenuously related to their namesake mentioned in the classic works of such writers as Pliny and Ptolemy. Their own third century belief, according to Ammianus, was that they were a people of mixed Germanic and Roman heritage that sprung up along the Roman borderlands, the *limes*, at the height of the Roman Empire. This may be more historically believable, though it must also be viewed with some reservation.

What was certain was that by the turn of the fifth century, the Burgundians were firmly situated on the

---

[1] Lucien Musset, *The Germanic Invasions: The Making of Europe AD 400-600*, trans. Edward and Columba James (University Park, Penn.: The Pennsylvania State University Press, 1975), 134.

Rhine and received the blessing of Rome to occupy and hold the region for the Empire. This first kingdom was a short-lived failure. The Burgundian's zealous expansion caused consternation in Rome and resulted in a vicious reaction from the Roman General Flavius Aëtius who, either singly or with the aid of the Huns, delivered a devastating blow to the fledgling Burgundian kingdom. These tragic events inspired the *Niebelungenlied*.

After seeing them sufficiently weakened, Aëtius thought enough of their prowess in battle to re-settle them in an area more beneficial to Rome. This second kingdom of the Burgundians originated in Sapaudia—somewhere around Lake Geneva in modern day Switzerland—and eventually expanded to include much of south-eastern Gaul. It was more successful than the first, probably because it was constructed and held by a family, the Gibichungs, led first by Gundioc and Chilperic I and then by Gundioc's son Gundobad, who continued to view it as land held for the greater Roman Empire, rather than as their own possession.[2]

Whether a fallacy or not, this enabled the Burgundian rulers to maintain continuity between the old provincial government and their new amalgamation and softened the changes felt by the Gallo-Romans. As a result, the Gallo-Roman inhabitants of the Burgundian protectorate seemed to have regarded the Burgundians

---

[2] *Avitus of Vienne: Letters and Selected Prose*, trans. with an introduction by Danuta Shanzer and Ian Wood, Translated Texts for Historians, vol. 38, (Liverpool: Liverpool University Press, 2002), 24-25. (Hereafter cited as *Avitus of Vienne*). Shanzer and Wood convincingly argue this case.

as the most desirable, or at the very least the most benign, of barbarian overlords.

The Burgundian's tepid Arianism also contributed to this impression, but the primary factor in the relative ease with which Gallo-Romans accepted Burgundian rule may have been a result of the Burgundian's long exposure to Rome and their adoption and familiarity with its social, political and cultural norms. In this, it was quite possible that the tenuous evidence of Roman blood in their veins, whether real or legend, had the affect of instilling in the Burgundians a sense of kinship to Rome and, by extension, the Gallo-Romans.

The Burgundians made accommodation for the rights of Romans in their laws, were tolerant of their religion and were relatively benevolent rulers.[3] The lack of written evidence that can be directly assigned to Burgundians, with the notable exception of the *Lex Gundobada*, could be attributed to the relative ease with which they adopted Roman culture, language and institutions and assimilated them into their own society. This also reveals that Burgundian society was not distinct

---

[3] Herwig Wolfram, *The Roman Empire and Its Germanic Peoples*, trans. Thomas Dunlap (Berkeley, Cal.: University of California Press, 1997), 249. Wolfram argues they accommodated out of necessity. "Burgundy was both a dream and a reality of European history. The power political basis of its own history, however, strikes me as astonishingly weak. Three generations of independent statehood, almost continuously threatened by setbacks and even destruction, is all that was granted to the Burgundians from the time they crossed the Rhine. Perhaps the resilience of the Burgundian tradition lay precisely in the fact that those who embodied it within Gaul had to represent a credible alternative to resist the powerful kingdoms in East and West."

enough and did not have strong enough traditions to maintain a unique character in the face of Roman culture. This ability to, at the least, embrace other societal structures or, at the most, lose their own cultural identity to them, contributed to their downfall.[4]

The Burgundians repeatedly accommodated other groups by allowing them to settle in Burgundy. Alamans already inhabited the lands around Geneva and the Jura Mountains when the Burgundians took control of the region as *foederati*. The *Lex Gundobad* stated that "all assimilable elements, Visigoths and even runaway slaves, should be accepted into the community."[5] Their attempts to accommodate many within their realm, which was so instrumental in initially maintaining internal peace, had the eventual effect of making enemies of many outside and inside their realm.

Despite the latitude they showed their Catholic subjects, the Arian Burgundian kings were reluctant to fully embrace Catholicism. Though some of the Burgundian royal family, particularly the women, were certainly Catholic, it was only after the ascension of Sigismund in A.D. 517 that a systematic dismantling of the Arian church within the Burgundian Kingdom

---

[4] Patrick Geary, *The Myth of Nations: The Medieval Origins of Europe* (Princeton, N.J.: Princeton University Press, 2002), 112-13, and 114, for his contention that "The Burgundians rapidly lost any cultural, religious, or genealogical identity they may ever have had, and , by the sixth century, Burgundian seems to have meant little more than the holder of lands that had originally been the military allotments divided among the barbarians."

[5] Musset, *Germanic Invasions*, 65.

occurred. It may have occurred too late. This apparent weakness of conviction may have already prompted Catholic ideologues within Burgundy to seek other, more convicted patrons. Or it at least provided them with the necessary political and religious cover to support regime change.

Clovis and his Franks purportedly used the Arianism of the Burgundians as an excuse to attack around A.D. 500, probably with the support of some Catholic bishops within Burgundy. Conversely, after the Burgundians had converted to Catholicism under Sigismund, the Ostrogothic King Theodoric used their apparent betrayal of Arianism (and a desire to exact revenge for Sigismund—Theodoric's son-in-law—having murdered Theodoric's grandson) as justification for a coordinated attack with the Franks who, according to Gregory of Tours, were seeking revenge on behalf of Queen Clotilda (a story that sprung up years after the actual events). Whatever the reasons given, the primary causes of the downfall of the Burgundian kingdom were not revenge, Sigismund's lapses in leadership nor Burgundian Arianism. Rather, it was the Burgundian kingdom's vulnerable geography between their more powerful and ambitious neighbors, the Franks and Goths.

Situated on lands straddling the Alps, the Burgundians were caught between Goths in the south and Franks to the north, both of whom were desirous of the rich Burgundian lands. Though religion and revenge may have only been convenient excuses for invasion, it is probable that the Burgundians eventually would have had to face either, or both, of its neighbors in armed conflict. Sigismund's own Catholicism and few charitable acts could not insulate him against those who opposed him.

For, regardless of his displayed piety, the murder of his own son—who also happened to be Theodoric's grandson—undoubtedly alienated many in the Church and, along with other actions, fomented doubts, and eventually possible rebellion, among the ecclesiastics and Gallo-Romans. Without their support, Sigismund was vulnerable to both internal strife and external invasion.

His death did not quiet the storm. In disarray, and despite the stubborn attempts of Sigismund's younger brother, Godomoar, to save it, the Burgundian Kingdom was ripe for conquest. The Franks and Goths obliged. Once defeated, the Burgundians vanished into the mists of time; consigned to the annals as just another victim of history. The obvious legacy of the Burgundians is the *Nibelungenlied*, their namesake region in France, and the wine produced there. Yet, their most important legacy is that left by the Burgundian princess Clotilda. Her marriage to Clovis was in some way related to one of the most significant royal religious conversions in history.

Whether Clotilda inspired Clovis' conversion directly or whether he was inspired for political reasons, their marriage enabled his acceptance by the Roman Catholic Church and set the stage for his emergence as the first powerful barbarian king religiously aligned with his Roman subjects. Clovis and his armies, with the valuable support of the Pope, conquered other peoples who also were—convenientyly—Arian Christians and thus safeguarded Catholic Christianity in the West.

This work focuses on the history of the Burgundians from the time they—or more correctly, a people of their name—emerged from Scandinavia until they were permanently rendered subjects of the Merovingian Franks in the early sixth century. It also includes a discussion of the historical interpretations of the origins of the Burgundians as well as other questions concerning their history. I've examined how and why the Burgundians entered Roman Gaul, the political and social nature of their short-lived kingdoms and their relationship with other entities, such as the Goths, Franks and Catholic church. Throughout, I've tried to give specific attention to how recent, more general, interpretations of Germanic society apply in particular to the Burgundians. Finally, I've covered the personal history and historical impact of prominent Burgundians, such as King Gundobad and Saint Clotilda, within the context of the larger Burgundian narrative.

Though both of the Burgundian kingdoms ultimately ended in failure, their second kingdom was more successful than the first. It provided an example of how disparate groups could survive and thrive if united under strong and able leadership, such as that provided by the militarily and politically astute Gundobad.

The Burgundian Kingdom that had developed by the

sixth century had many traditional Germanic characteristics, but it also successfully integrated both Roman culture and societal institutions. The intermixing of Gallo-Romans, Christians and Germans resulted in an amalgamated Romano-Burgundian kingdom that had laws for all and tolerated two forms of Christianity. This Burgundian kingdom briefly foreshadowed the culture—more famously realized in the age of Charlemagne—that would eventually emerge in Western Europe.

CHAPTER 1
BURGUNDIAN ORIGINS AND EARLY MIGRATION
(c.500 B.C. to 100 A.D.)

Early Interpretations of Burgundian Origins

So where did the Burgundians come from? For that matter, where did other Germanic tribes originate? Entire forests have been pulped so that historians could attempt to answer those questions. Understandably, it's easier to supply a general answer regarding the origins of those whom we call the Germanic people. But devils are in details, especially when trying to parse out the origins of one particular group. Yet, historians have seemingly always—and continue to--try!

Pliny the Elder mentioned the *Burgodiones* in his *Natural History*, written in the first century, sometime before A.D. 79. Pliny believed that these "Burgodiones" were members of the "Vandal race" of Germans and placed them near the Oder and Vistula rivers. Later, Ptolemy, in his *Geography* of about A.D. 150, wrote of the *Burguntae*, who lived between the Suevus and the Vistula rivers. A few centuries later, Jordanes, in his *History of the Goths*, mentioned the Burgundians, claiming that Fastida, King of the Gepidae, had nearly destroyed them near the Vistula (as we'll see later, he

11

probably had it backwards). These early writers attempted to classify Germans by using either a geographical system, as did Pliny and Ptolemy, or a combination of this with a mythical or genealogical system, as did the late 1st/early 2nd century A.D. Roman historian Tacitus.[6]

Historians in the nineteenth and early twentieth centuries utilized the latest in linguistic knowledge to examine the evidence and determined that the name of a Swedish island, Bornholm, located in the Baltic Sea east of Denmark, south of Sweden, and north of Poland, was a shortened form of Burgundarholm. This, they concluded, was clearly the ancestral *holm* of the Burgundians.[7] In addition to this linguistic evidence,

---

[6] See Pliny, *Natural History*, trans. H. Rackham, Loeb Classical Library (Cambridge, Mass.: Harvard University Press, 1942), 2:195, 197; and Ptolemy, *Geography of Claudius Ptolemy*, trans. and ed. Edward Luther Stevenson (New York: New York Public Library, 1932; reprint, New York: Dover Books, 1991), available at <http://www.ukans.edu/history/index/ europe/ancient_rome/E/Gazetteer/Periods/Roman /Texts/Ptolemy/2/ 10/home.html>, 19 Nov 03, (3/19/2004); and Jordanes, *The Origins and Deeds of the Goths*. trans. Charles C. Mierow [book on-line] (Princeton, N.J.: Princeton University Press, 1915); available at www.northvegr.org/lore/pdf/ jordanes.pdf> (19 March 2004); and Tacitus, *Germania*, in *Tacitus*, trans. Maurice Hutton and rev. E.H.Warmington, vol. 1, *Agricola, Germania, Dialogus*, Loeb Classical Series (Cambridge, Mass.: Harvard University Press, 1914. Reprint 1970), 131-137; and Musset, *Germanic Invasions*, 7.

[7] For examples of this type of philological investigation, see George Hempl, "The Linguistic and Ethnografic Status of the Burgundians," *Transactions and Proceedings of the American Philological Association* 39 (1908): 105-19; and Kemp Malone, "Ptolemy's Skandia," *The American Journal of Philology* 45, no.4 (1924): 362-70, for the argument Scandinavian toponyms, like Borgundarholm, could be derived from a number of other sources and thus mean something other than a place where a people called the Burgundians once lived, see Walter Goffart, *Barbarians and Romans,*

historians interpreted written sources and oral tradition such that they placed the Burgundians among those East German tribes that migrated from Scandinavia toward the Vistula during the first century. This confirmed the location of the Burgundians as portrayed in the writings of Pliny, Tacitus, Ptolemy, and Jordanes.[8]

Archeological evidence seemed to confirm or modify these beliefs. The use of archeology to supplement the writing of history came to the fore in the 1880s, led by German historians.[9] The centerpiece of their theory was an idea of ethnic homogeneity that allowed them to link specific archeological finds with particular people mentioned in the classic works of Pliny, Tacitus, and others, as well as the work of the contemporary philologists. In the years immediately following World War II, an understandable reaction occurred against this nationalistic, ethnically

---

A.D. 418-584: The Techniques of Accommodation (Princeton: Princeton University Press, 1980), 17-19.

[8] Jordanes, *Goths*, 17; J.B. Bury, *The Invasion of Europe by the Barbarians* (New York: W.W. Norton & Company, 1967; reprint, New York: W.W. Norton & Company, 2000), 15 (page citations are to the reprint edition); Robert Latouche, *Caesar to Charlemagne: The Beginnings of France*, trans. Jennifer Nicholson (London: Phoenix House, 1968), 166; Malcolm Todd. *The Northern Barbarians: 100 B.C.-A.D. 300*. (London: Hutchinson University Library, 1975), 20-23.

[9] See Todd, *The Northern Barbarians*, 20-21, which also explained that these historians were led by Gustav Kossinna., whose theories were considered the standard treatment of the subject until World War II. Kossinna's method convinced himself and others that the Germans had been an ethnically homogenous people from the Bronze Age through the Roman Iron Age. This was a product of the nationalism that swept Europe in the nineteenth century and used nefariously by the Third Reich during the Second World War.

homogenous interpretation.

However, during this initial backlash, some critics went too far in not recognizing any sort of Germanic culture prior to 100 B.C. It has since been determined that a definite, Germanic material culture can be traced to the northern Iron Age of the fifth and fourth centuries B.C. The concept of an ethnically and culturally united Germanic people is still debated,[10] though the various "Germanic people" did share some common traits. Nonetheless, the idea that specific tribes of Germanic people can be identified by archeology (ie; grave goods) alone continues to be met with skepticism.

Characteristics of Early Germanic Society

In general, archeological findings have indicated that the Germanic people living east of the Rhine were primarily pastoral and not nomadic (like the people of the Eurasian steppes) because the climate of Germany did not necessitate such movement. They did not spend all of their time tending herds as they also hunted and farmed to supplement their diet of meat, milk, and cheese.[11] The settlements that existed in *Germania* during this time ranged from the small, single farm to a

---

[10] Todd, *The Northern Barbarians*, 20-21.

[11] E.A. Thompson, "The Germans in the Time of Caesar," in *The Barbarian Invasions: Catalyst of a New Order*, ed. Katherine Fischer Drew, (New York: Holt, Rinehart and Winston, 1970), 71; Goffart, *Barbarians and Romans*, 28-29; Patrick Geary, *Before France and Germany: The Creation and Transformation of the Merovingian World* (New York: Oxford University Press, 1988), 51; and Todd, *The Northern Barbarians*, 116-17, stated that archaeological evidence does not support the idea that the Germans were semi-nomadic.

group of farms situated in what would best be described as a village. Archeologists and historians have determined that the "overriding impression conveyed by the excavated sites is of stable and enduring communities, some occupying the same sites for many decades or even centuries, others shifting their dwellings without moving far beyond their original confines."[12]

They were not entirely dependent, or socially defined by, their possession of animals, though it was their primary means of subsistence and source of prestige, dignity and wealth. Cattle were the most important livestock, but geography and environment determined whether sheep or pigs were the second most important.[13] They were also farmers, and barley, oats and rye were the most common grains, while vegetables and herbs were also cultivated. Additionally, fruits, such as apples, berries and grapes were gathered, though not cultivated.[14] Thus, with the ability to raise, grow, or gather a wide array of food, and the ability to barter for food they couldn't produce on their own, the Germanic economy was able to support fairly large communities, much like the neighboring western Roman provinces.[15]

---

[12] Todd, *The Northern Barbarians*, 116.

[13] See Todd, *The Northern Barbarians*, 117-21, for a concise discussion of the types of livestock kept by the Germans.

[14] Todd, *The Northern Barbarians*, 121-23.

[15] See Todd, *The Northern Barbarians*, 131-32, which observed that, since there is hardly any evidence of Roman influence on German agriculture, it is understandable why the Germans were able to adapt well when they settled in these provinces.

Rings and brooches with gold filigree provide evidence of Germans working in gold dating from the mid-first century B.C. to the beginning of the first century A.D. Germans preferred Roman silver to gold and there is evidence of them working in silver that dates to roughly the same period. While working in these precious metals was important to the Germans, and was perhaps more importantly of interest to the Romans, the Germans viewed iron-working as the most important craft of all.

While evidence has been found of large iron manufacturing centers, most iron was produced in smaller quantities by local smiths. Thus, Tacitus' assertion that "iron is not plentiful among them"[16] seems to have been derived from ignorance rather than fact.[17] Salt was also an important commodity and was often the object of tribal conflict. Pottery, wood-working, textiles and leather were also important industries. In all of these areas, Germanic technology progressed in fits and starts, often stagnating in isolated spots or progressing rapidly in others.[18]

Human and animal sacrifice was practiced, with mostly domesticated livestock serving as the ritualistic object, though dogs and wild animals also were used. The animals were eaten in sacrificial meals, with the remains often deposited in bogs.[19] "The prominence of

[16] Tacitus, *Germania*, 139.
[17] Todd, *The Northern Barbarians*, 134-49.
[18] Ibid., 149-56.
[19] Ibid., 197-98.

the horse in the animal sacrifices deserves special notice. Commonly only the skull, tail and feet are represented....This rite of burying the skull and extremities of the skeleton links the Germanic world with the Baltic regions and the Steppes."[20]

The dog appears to have been the most sacrificed animal in many regions, though there is no evidence that any portion of the dog was eaten in a ritualistic meal. These canine sacrifices may have been linked to a fertility cult, although it could also have served as a substitute for a man as skeletons of both often occur in the same archeological digs. Evidence of human sacrifice exists, mostly among prisoners that were sacrificed to war gods, though there were other rituals that seemed to require human sacrifice to different gods.[21]

Women were considered valuable contributors to Germanic society as they "provided a network of kinship ties" and "gave inspirational support and were nurturers and providers."[22] Women were responsible for housework and at least some helped to plow fields. According to Tacitus, the wives of the barbarians went to battle to support their husbands by tending cookfires, bringing food and offering general encouragement. The

---

[20] Ibid., 199.

[21] Todd, *The Northern Barbarians*, 199-203, stated that the corpses found in the bogs of northern Europe have provided much evidence in this area. It could be that, much like the ancient Egyptians who buried their cats with them, perhaps the Germans buried their dogs for companionship in the afterlife.

[22] Suzanne Fonay Wemple, *Women in Frankish Society: Marriage and the Cloister 500 to 900*, (Philadelphia: University of Pennsylvania Press, 1981), 11.

historian Ammianus claimed that some of these wives also fought.[23] Tacitus also said that the Germans "conceive that in woman is a certain uncanny and prophetic sense: and so they neither scorn to consult them nor slight their answers"[24] and that they revered many women ancestors.[25]

German marriage was not a "legal relationship" but "an arrangement, accepted as social fact, whereby a man cohabitated with a woman for the purposes of copulation, procreation, and the division of labor."[26] Gender was the main determinant of labor: men were warriors while women raised the children, worked the fields and took care of the home. In Germanic society, it was considered a mother's duty to provide the primary example and instruction in religious and moral matters. As a result, it was the Germanic women, be they mothers, grandmothers, or aunts, who played a key role in the upbringing of Germanic males when they were most impressionable.[27]

The largest portion of the population was comprised of the free men. The number of cattle or swine they held determined their status in the community and they exhibited their freedom by joining in warfare. Generally, it was a patriarchal society and

---

[23] Tacitus, *Germany*, 143; and Ammianus Marcellinus, *The Surviving Books of the History*, trans. John C. Rolfe, *Ammianus Marcellinus*, Loeb Classical Library (Cambridge, Mass.: Harvard University Press, 1939), 1:195.

[24] Tacitus, *Germania*, 143.

[25] Ibid.

[26] Wemple, *Women in Frankish Society*, 12.

[27] Ibid., 12, 59.

households combined into a larger group, or clan. The unifying factors of the clan were twofold, internal and external. Internally, the clan provided a basic form of law that kept the peace among its members. Externally, the members united into greater groups, the largest called tribes, to participate in feuds with other groups. [28]

The tribe was composed of both paternal and maternal kin groups who believed in a shared common ancestry and strengthened internal bonds by viewing internal fighting within a clan as an unforgivable crime. Thus, peace was maintained internally and was additionally fostered by focusing aggression upon external enemies by requiring a certain degree of obligation toward a common defense and participating in feuds to assist other members of one's tribe. However, membership within these larger groups was very tenuous as individuals and their families could join one group or another based on other kin relations or upon which group met their particular needs at a given time. Thus, the most important functional unit of barbarian society was the family, not the clan, or tribe.[29]

Families composed villages, led by a group of free men led by a headman, or chief, who may have been determined based on a variety of attributes, including, but not limited to, wealth, ancestry, family connections or influence in the larger group of kindred, "the people" or *gentes*, of which his village was a part. The villages that made up these *gentes* "were bound together by a

---

[28] Geary, *Before France and Germany,* 52-55.
[29] Geary, *The Myth of Nations*, 73-74.

combination of religious, legal, and political traditions that imparted a strong, if unstable, sense of unity."[30] Ancestry myths were based on the lives and exploits of heroes, who were seen as divine founders of a *gentes*. The tales of revenge, war, blood feud and kinship helped groups of Germans to unite because of a sense of shared ancestry to a specific individual.[31]

The Germanic tribes were led by two sorts of kings--one religious and the other military. These men ruled the tribe by a complicated mixture of single or joint rule, dependent upon the particular situation in which the tribe found itself. The first type of chief, identified as being more religious in nature, was the *thiudans*. He belonged to a traditional royal family that was associated with the mythic, historical and cultural origins of the tribe and was a symbol of tribal stability.

In time of war, military authority was given to the martial, usually non-royal leader, called a *dux* (or general) by Tacitus. These leaders presided over the Germanic council of free warriors, called a *Thing*. The organization of a *Thing* varied, but in general, it gathered

---

[30] Ibid., 74.

[31] Geary, *The Myth of Nations*, 74, and also see 74-75 for the explanation that some historians believe that the royal families were those primarily associated with the particular myths of a group. It is also possible that different families had other traditions and stories and attempted to impose these as preeminent over those of other families. Such stories and traditions were also probably more dispersed throughout a society than being seen as the sole property of one family. If this is so, then Geary asserted that, during the fourth and fifth centuries, when certain individuals emerged as tribal leaders, they and their families became associated, or they claimed for themselves, the traditional myths and stories of the tribe.

to judge its members, discuss war, and to formulate tribal policy.

The *Thing* was the core of the fundamental idea of kindred, or *gentes*, which was the basis of Germanic society. Yet, tribes were constantly in flux as every disruption of internal or external peace could result in a splintered clan and new clans reformed along different lines. This natural state of tribal ebb and flow was exacerbated by contact with the Roman Empire, which intensified both kinds of disruption.[32]

Characteristics of Early Germanic Migrations

Although it has been generally accepted that the Germans moved from their original lands, the reasons for which they did so continues to be debated. The most questionable early historical discussions centered on attempts to pinpoint the specific migratory path of certain Germanic tribes.[33] Originally, historians believed that the Burgundians were among what came to be classified as the East Germans. These tribes left their lands beyond the Elbe River in the third and fourth centuries in search of new lands on a journey that took them towards the Black Sea and the Danube. Historians

---

[32] Geary, *Before France and Germany,* 55.

[33] Wolfram, *Germanic Peoples*, 4, offered the pithy comment that "[d]ebates concerning the Germanic identity of the Germanic tribes who lived east of the Rhine fill entire libraries."; and C.R. Whittaker, *Frontiers of the Roman Empire: A Social and Economic Study* (Baltimore: The Johns Hopkins University Press, 1994), 212, who cautioned that "[w]e have to break away from the stereotypes of 'tribal' history and mass movements of tribal migration, which, when we can trace them archaeologically...seem to be slow movements of infiltration by small groups of warriors."

hypothesized that growing population and a related need for better food resources, as well as migratory pressure from other tribes, were probably the motivating factors in East German migration.[34] These theories are still generally sound, though the attempt to specify migratory paths has been criticized.[35]

More recent scholarship has relied primarily on archeological evidence and has re-classified the Burgundians as Elbe Germans.[36] Their appearance in written sources clearly indicates that a Germanic tribe known as Burgundians existed, though their specific

---

[34] Examples of this traditional theory are in Bury, *Invasion of Europe*, 15-16; and Edward Gibbon, *The Decline and Fall of the Roman Empire*, Great Books of the Western World, vol.40-41 (Chicago: Encyclopedia Britannica, 1952), 698. Both Gibbon and Bury thought the wars fought by Marcus Aurelius during the end of the second century provided evidence for the movement of the East Germans because, the concluded, the barbarians Aurelius fought had been displaced by migrating East Germans.

[35] See Goffart *Barbarians and Romans*, 19-20, which asserted that, while early Burgundian migrations are obvious, it is questionable to use tenuous evidence to interpolate their exact movements; and also see Wolfram, *Germanic Peoples*, 8, who discounted the role of hunger or desire for goods as motivation for the migrations and instead attributed pressure from constant warfare within barbarian society. This constant warfare was a direct result of "the driving force of tribal life [which] was the pathos of heroism. Barbarian traditions are the tales of the 'deeds of brave men'— only the warrior matters; tribe and army are one."

[36] For the classification of Elbe Germans see Geary, *Before France and Germany*, 51; and see Wolfram, *Germanic Peoples*, 259, who noted that linguists used to consider the Burgundians as East Germans, but are no longer so sure. The Burgundians were traditionally classified as a Gothic people, but this may have been because they were Arian Christians. Sidonius himself considered them to be Germanic, not Goths, a classification that a contemporary ethnographer would not confuse, according to Wolfram.

migration route remains unknown.[37] An analysis of the few Burgundian remains, primarily skulls, indicated characteristics similar to those of people of Asiatic origin. Additionally, some historians have detected Asiatic themes and styles in the artwork of various Germanic tribes, including the Burgundians, during the migration period.[38] Other archeological evidence taken from the area around the lower Vistula--traditionally believed to be a home to the Burgundians--indicated that the region experienced a population loss towards the end of the third century. Some historians took this as evidence of a western migration of the Burgundians at this time. However, this by itself is not enough to determine Burgundians' specific migratory path.[39]

---

[37] This was noted earlier by Malcolm Todd, *Everyday Life of The Barbarians: Goths, Franks, and Vandals*. (New York: Dorset Press, 1972), 8-9. Todd believed it impossible to link a tribe mentioned by Tacitus and others of that era with so-called "archeological cultures" and most modern archeologists "prefer to leave on one side questions concerning the ethnic significance of archeological mater." Todd placed the Burgundians among an eastern group of Germans, living between the Oder and Vistula, with the Goths, Vandals and Rugii.

[38] Musset, *Germanic Invasions*, 13-14, which mentioned that analysis of Burgundian skulls indicated Asian characteristics. Additionally, Musset pointed out that it had been conjectured that the second part of the name of a later king, Gundiocus (Gundioc), showed Hunnic influence, 65; and Herbert Kuhn, "Asiatic Influences on the Art of the Migrations," *Parnassus* 9, no.1 (1937): 13-16, 43.

[39] Todd, *The Northern Barbarians*, 91-92; and also see Patrick Geary, "A poisoned Landscape: Ethnicity and Nationalism in the Nineteenth Century," in *The Myth of Nations*, 15-40, for a substantive recounting of the problems associated with relying on nineteenth century interpretations of the history of the Germanic tribes from the time of Caesar to the migration period. Geary detailed how the compilation of the MGH lay at the root of many of these problems as its composition relied heavily on the science of

philology which resulted in classifying people according to a language family, from which tribal nationalities were then developed.

CHAPTER 2
BURGUNDIAN CONTACT WITH THE ROMAN EMPIRE
(C.100 A.D. TO 400 A.D.)

Burgundians along the Limes

Though their early history has remained clouded, Burgundian contact with Rome has enabled a better understanding of how Burgundian society evolved. After initial attempts during the first and early second century to penetrate beyond the Rhine and Danube, Rome created an artificial frontier, the *limes*, between the empire and the barbarians. This frontier stretched from the Rhine north of Koblenz to the Danube valley near Regensburg. Barbarians settled the area immediately to the east of the limes, perhaps under a treaty with Rome.[40] The Romans also saw the importance of rivers in connecting Rome with this frontier.

While historians once thought that the rivers formed a sort of border, it has become recognized that these rivers were not political limits but the outer limit

---

[40] Todd, *The Northern Barbarians*, 31; also see Stephen L. Dyson, *The Creation of the Roman Frontier*, (Princeton , N.J.: Princeton University Press, 1985), for a survey of the development of the Roman frontier and border control policies of the Roman Empire from the early fourth century B.C. to the mid-first century B.C.

of logistical support for the empire. The forts on rivers such as the Danube and Rhine were supply depots, not defensive installations,[41] though they would sometimes serve that purpose. Thus, the *limes* served less as a barrier to barbarian invasion, and more as a "free trade zone" shared with the barbarians. It was indeed a frontier rather than a border. The rivers were the avenue by which needed supplies were sent to support the Roman army and to trade with the barbarians. Supply was necessary because the surrounding lands were not sufficient to support the Roman army.[42]

The *limes* were the areas in which the greatest amount of commerce between the Romans and barbarians occurred. Exposure to Roman culture through trade resulted in a fundamental change in Germanic society.[43] Rome believed trade was a stabilizing force that could civilize the barbarians.

---

[41] Whittaker, *Frontiers of the Roman Empire*, 99.

[42] Ibid., 101-104.

[43] C.D. Gordon, "Subsidies in Roman Imperial Defence," *Phoenix* 3, no.2 (1949): 67-68, noted that the effects of this trade were also felt by the Roman Empire. "Of considerable interest are the effects which this policy had on external trade and the internal economy of the Empire, and on the barbarians who received the subsidies. Recent history has many examples of trade agreements by which one government has lent or given large sums to another government for purposes that will benefit both. The Canadian and American credits and loans to Europe have not been made in a spirit of pure philanthropy, but with the idea, among others, of stimulating the home industries by providing purchasing power for local products in foreign countries. Without imagining that Rome ever paid subsidies with this in mind, we can see that the sending of Roman money to foreigners must have helped the Roman export trade, especially to the barbarian north which had so great a need for Roman manufactures."

Roman leadership hoped that the barbarians would come to rely and value Roman goods to the extent that any disruption in trade, such as by raids or war, would end. Apart from trade, Roman policy also allowed for the liberal dispensing of gifts to achieve the desired results. These Roman policies of trading and gift-giving were followed with three goals in mind: "to buy alliance and active military help against more formidable enemies; to buy immunity from attack; and to create division among the enemies of the empire so as to maintain the frontiers intact."[44] In accomplishing these goals the policy was, at least initially, successful.

The trade and subsidies had the desirable economic effects on the Germanic people. The Germans along the borderlands became accustomed to the quality of Roman goods and they also converted to a money economy. Cassius Dio, governor on the Danube in the early third century A.D. remarked:

> The barbarians were adapting themselves to the Roman world. They were setting up markets and peaceful meetings, although they had not forgotten their ancestral habits, their tribal customs, their independent life, and the freedom that came from weapons. However, as long as they learned these different habits

---

[44] Gordon, "Subsidies in Roman Imperial Defence," 60, in which it was also noted that the practice grew "in importance until it became the main defence [sic] of the frontiers."

gradually and under some sort of supervision, they did not find it difficult to change their life, and they were becoming different without realizing it.[45]

In turn, they brought this new style of trade to the Germans deeper in the interior. The result was a slow cultural "equalizing" between the Germanic peoples along the *limes* and those in the interior.[46]

The Roman trade policy did gradually establish a certain, albeit inconsistent, cultural equivalency between the Empire and the barbarians. However, it also caused conflict within individual tribes as both competition for favors from Rome and between pro- and anti-Roman factions splintered old tribes and formed new ones based on relationships to Rome. These factions resorted to violence to press their case, some at the behest of Rome, which had the money so desirable to barbarian leaders.[47] These leaders held, or desired, political power that was acquired and reinforced through their ability to control trade in their region.[48]

Thus, the result of Roman and barbarian

---

[45] *Cassius Dio*, 56.18.2, in Whittaker, *Frontiers of the Roman Empire*, 131.

[46] Gordon, "Subsidies in Roman Imperial Defence," 69.

[47] See Geary, *Before France and Germany*, 57-59; Goffart, *Barbarians and Romans*, 5-6; and Ralph Whitney Mathisen, *Roman Aristocrats in Barbarian Gaul: Strategies for Survival in an Age of Transition* (Austin: University of Texas Press, 1993), 1-2.

[48] Whittaker, *Frontiers of the Roman Empire*, 130 and 262. "It is reasonable to conclude that soldiers, particularly officers, on active service became increasingly powerful locally through their attachment to the land in the regions where they served."

interaction along the *limes* was a destabilization. Rome, with her money and political power, enabled some chiefs to gain riches previously unimagined. More importantly, these chiefs were trained in the politics and economics of Rome and were able apply these principles successfully among their tribes. At the same time, those barbarian groups not embraced by Rome often grouped into large confederations and wreaked havoc along the borderlands. These new groups formed and re-formed continually, some around a strong, Romanized barbarian and others around a particular leader at the head of a barbarian confederation. These new "tribes" often associated themselves with much older traditions for the sake of unity and continuity.[49]

The incessant barbarian conflicts that occurred during the latter part of the second century increased the importance of the military leaders in the tribes. These *reiks* often attributed their military prowess as "a sign of the gods' favor," which enabled them to "add a religious aura to their position."[50] The god Tiwaz was a war god, influential on the battlefield, but was also more importantly the god of law and order and was associated with the Germanic *Thing*, the essential governing body of a traditional tribe.[51]

As the tribe began to identify itself less with its land of origin, it also de-emphasized the role of the god

---

[49] Geary, *The Myth of Nations*, 78.

[50] Ibid., 61.

[51] Todd, *The Northern Barbarians*, 84, "One of [Tiwaz's] titles used on inscriptions set up in the Roman Provinces was *Mars Thingsus*, indicating a connection with the Thing or people's assembly."

Marc A. Comtois

Tiwaz, and the *thiudans*, and identified itself more with the new, successful war leader and the corresponding god of war, Woden. "Victories created new traditions,"[52] and, regardless of race, language, or political origin, if an individual fought alongside a certain war leader, he was a member of that war leader's tribe.[53] The Marcomannic Wars were evidence of "a radical restructuring of the Germanic world"[54] and "the last decades of the second century were the most vital period of ethnogenesis in Germanic history."[55]

Barbarians had been used by Rome for her armies almost from their first exposure to the Empire. Caesar used Germanic troops during his Gaul campaign. Initially serving as separate, tribe-based auxiliary forces, they were eventually merged into the general Roman auxiliary forces. Some were picked to be special body guards for the emperor, which formed an important political counterweight to the Praetorian Guard. Most

---

[52] Geary, *Before France and Germany*, 61.

[53] Geary, *Before France and Germany*, 61; and Todd, *The Northern Barbarians*, 182-84, who noted that sources crucial to understanding Germanic religion and ritual are sparse and often contradictory. The literary sources are often too random and too concentrated on the more sensational myths to be taken as a comprehensive explanation of Germanic religion. Nonetheless, writers have focused on the war gods at the expense of the more peaceful gods or those associated with life and regeneration.

[54] Geary, *Before France and Germany*, 60.

[55] Geary, *Before France and Germany*, 61; and see Whittaker, *Frontiers of the Roman Empire*, 212-213, who called attention to the fact that "The terms 'Goths'—similar to 'Franks' [freemen] and 'Alamans' [all-men]—is a generic term meaning 'men' and gives a false impression of unity to what was basically a society fragmented into subdivisions that rapidly disintegrated after rare shows of unity."

important were the Germanic leaders who learned the Roman way of war and brought their knowledge back to their tribes.[56]

Barbarian war-leaders also identified themselves as both members of barbarian society and Roman officers and often used one position to advance the other. Some, such as Arbogast, used their position as Roman generals to marshal the necessary forces to attack their barbarian rivals, as Arbogast did by attacking Marcomer and Sunno across the Rhine. However, most often, accepting a high position in the Roman army usually meant forfeiting tribal political power.[57]

Roman money was important, especially to the barbarian leader, because victory alone could not maintain a king's prestige against other leaders in the tribe. Money equaled power, and Rome had a seemingly endless supply of the former. In exchange for money, barbarian kings provided Rome with military manpower. They used Roman money and booty acquired while pursuing Roman military ventures to satisfy their supporters and attract more warriors to their tribe. As such, military leaders did not rely solely on strict tribal bonds to attract warriors. Warrior bands, called *comitatus*, were based on personal loyalty to a leader rather than tribal bonds, and these became prevalent and added to the confusion among tribal society.[58]

---

[56] Todd, *The Northern Barbarians*, 33-34.

[57] Geary, *The Myth of Nations*, 84-85.

[58] Geary, *Before France and Germany* 62, 56-57.

Often, individual members of these bands participated in raids against tribes with whom their ancestral tribe was ostensibly at peace. This in turn caused more widespread conflict. Also, when a tribe moved, and inevitably encountered and fought other tribes, a natural upward social mobility occurred within its ranks as warriors proved themselves on the battlefield. Skill was prime, not ethnic or social background, and those that distinctly exhibited these characteristics emerged as leaders. This near-constant state of warfare resulted in the splintering and reformation of tribes, often with a war leader and his *comitatus* serving as the nucleus for a new tribe. The war leaders of these new or reformed tribes called upon their own tribal heritage to provide an identity for their new tribe, often recycling remembered and revered tribal names to add an air of authenticity and respect.[59]

The Romans did not recruit barbarians for only military purposes. They also settled them on their lands to provide a needed workforce in regions that had been ravaged of their former population by war or famine. These barbarians, usually refugees were usually those who had themselves been defeated in war and were either held by the Romans or had asked the emperor for permission to settle on Roman lands. In exchange, these groups paid tribute and lived under Roman law, though

---

[59] Geary, *Before France and Germany*, 53; and see Musset, *Germanic Invasions*, 176, for the theory that the mixed nature of these peoples "must have brought about confrontations within each people, causing them to modify their institutions, and thus paving the way for an eventual reconciliation with the Romans."

they were not considered to be freemen and were subject to the emperor's whim. "Privileges could not be accorded to those whose origin lay beyond the boundaries of the Roman state."[60] Thus, barbarian workers in the Roman Empire helped to convert uncultivated land into cultivated and taxable land and provided manpower for other endeavors, such as mining.[61]

This constant state of societal flux as tribes formed, splintered, and re-formed both within and outside of lands under imperial control has revealed that tribes "were more processes than stable structures."[62] In essence, the tribes were similar to modern political parties. Each exalted a founding father, or concept, and included people and families of different ethnic stock, but shared cultural values. Additionally, given the inability of the Germans to act in concert at the tribal level, the traditional belief that they had acted in concert to raid the Roman Empire *en masse* has been shown as incorrect.[63]

---

[60] See Miroslava Mirkovic, "The Later Roman Colonate and Freedom," *Transactions of the American Philosophical Society* 87, no.2 (1997): 85. Mirkovic also made the point that "[t]he distribution of captive barbarians to landowners is indisputably confirmed as early as Diocletian's reign, in the Panegyric to Constantius I in 287 A.D.; the Life of Aurelianus in H[istoria] A[ugusta] probably also treats the same practice.", 99.

[61] Mirkovic, "Later Roman Colonate and Freedom," 98; and Whittaker, *Frontiers of the Roman Empire*, 223.

[62] Geary, *Before France and Germany*, 53.

[63] Geary, *Before France and Germany*, 39-41. Geary argued that the Romans applied a faulty template to the Germanic tribes in an attempt to put a familiar societal structure over the chaotic Germanic tribal world,

Evolution of Barbarian Arms and Tactics

During the first and second centuries A.D., the Germanic armies were primarily made up of foot soldiers armed with lances, spears, shields and only a few swords. Some Eastern Germans also probably used the axe. Very little body armor or helmets were worn. Most warriors fought naked or in little clothing and often wore just trousers or a short tunic and shoes. A shield was often carried and was used as both an offensive and a defensive weapon. Horses were not prevalent, and were used mostly by those tribes nearer to the Roman frontier than in the interior. However, even though most tribes lacked cavalry, their infantry prized speed above all else as an essential tactic against the more heavily armored Romans. During the first two centuries of contact

---

which strengthened the perception that Germans were both similar and even united in action; Goffart, in *Barbarians and Romans*, 12-13, concluded that this faulty theory of united Germanic action led to the belief that Germanic tribes consciously set out to set up kingdoms on Roman soil and these mistaken assumptions contributed to the flawed motif of Barbarian Invasions. It also implied that a single, united German entity opposed the Roman Empire and that both entities were conscious of being on opposing sides; and see Peter Heather, in "The Huns and the End of the Roman Empire in Western Europe," *The English Historical Review* 110, no.435 (1995): 37-8, 41. Heather concluded that, while the independent Germanic tribes didn't act in concert to attack the Roman Empire, the widespread displacement caused by the Huns effectively produced this effect; Wolfram, *Germanic Peoples*, 8, for the observation on political mobility through a tribal hierarchy; and Todd, *The Northern Barbarians*, 212, who observed that while "the history of the Germanic peoples in the fourth and fifth centuries, particularly in western Europe, is inextricably bound up with that of the declining Roman provinces... the tale is by no means always one of destruction and waste. Barbarians were by this time better equipped for life inside the empire than most ancient writers believed."

between the Germans and Rome there was little change in Germanic armament or tactics.[64]

From the time of the Marcomannic Wars (166 to 180 A.D.), however, changes began to take place. Roman types of equipment acquired as booty or because of service in the Roman army became more prevalent amongst the Germans. Use of axes and bows and arrows also increased. Swords were common and German smiths often copied captured Roman swords, especially the long, double-edged *spatha* and the shorter, broad *gladius*. Roman swords were also imported more at the beginning of the third century, especially into the region between the Oder and Vistula rivers.[65]

The barbarians were not well-schooled in siege warfare and lacked the knowledge to build adequate siege weapons. From the third century B.C. to the second century A.D., Germanic weaponry evolved little. Increasing contact with Rome changed that. By the fourth century, the armament of the Romans and Germans were often indistinguishable, largely because the Roman army itself was largely composed of Germans. Finally, while weapons and armor did change, the hit and run tactics of the ambush and the quick raid on a weak target were still preferred by the tribes.[66]

Thus, the first phase of the "barbarian invasions," which implied a violent struggle "between the civilized

---

[64] Todd, *Northern Barbarians*, 170-72, 174.
[65] Ibid., 175-76.
[66] Ibid., 178-80.

Roman citizens of the provinces and uncivilized intruders from outside the empire,"[67] were in actuality a slow merging of peoples along the border. There were battles, but these were as much between each other as they were against Roman settlements. Eventually, along the *limes*, the members of the two groups, Roman and German, were nearly indistinguishable from each other, with the Romans assuming many characteristics of the Germans. This has been supported by archeological evidence. Grave goods found in and near the frontier were similar to others found in the graves of Saxons, Franks and Alamani beyond the frontier. There was an especially marked similarity in the brooches discovered in women's graves from both regions.[68]

The various belts, buckles and military insignia discovered indicate an obvious link to Rome. Further, the inclusion of weapons in the graves seem to be only in those burials of people within the Empire and not among external Germans. This indicates a frontier culture of people "associated with Romans, possibly through military service."[69] Additionally, by the third century, legions, including the many barbarians in them, could marry legally (though many had informally for quite some time) and many, if not most, of their wives were drawn from the local population. This facilitated the assimilation of soldiers into specific localities.[70]

---

[67] Whittaker, *Frontiers of the Roman Empire*, 132.

[68] Ibid., 132-33, 235.

[69] Ibid., 235.

[70] Geary, *The Myth of Nations*, 72.

Two conclusions can be made, first "the change was not sudden" [71] and second the barbarians and the Romans dwelling on the *limes* had more in common than previously thought. Even children's graves contained swords and other martial implements and it is probable that not all of the graves were of Germans, "since in Gaul many of these burials appear to be perfectly integrated in provincial communities, using the same graveyards without signs of disruption."[72] Archeology has also revealed that "the settlements of Visigoths, Franks, and Burgundians in the fifth century, which [were] marked on maps, are really not distinguishable in terms of new cultures coming into Gaul from beyond the frontiers." [73]

End of the Limes

The Rhine-Danube *limes* was short-lived, though it withstood the Marcomannic Wars of A.D. 166-175 and A.D. 178-180.[74] When not trading with the Romans, the Germans were less concerned with destroying the frontiers of the Rhine and Danube than with raiding the

---

[71] Whittaker, *Frontiers of the Roman Empire*, 237.

[72] Ibid., 235.

[73] Edward James, "The Merovingian archaeology of south-west Gaul," *British Archaeological Reports, Suppl. Series* 25, (Oxford, 1977): 61 and maps on 244, in Whittaker, *Frontiers of the Roman Empire*, 233; and Chris Wickham, *Early Medieval Italy: Central Power and Local Society 400-1000* , (Totowa, N.J., 1981), 68, in Geary, *The Myth of Nations*, 39, who warned that "[a] man or woman with a Lombard-style brooch is no more necessarily a Lombard than a family in Bradford with a Toyota is Japanese; artifacts are no secure guide to ethnicity."

[74] Todd, *Northern Barbarians*, 31.

lands beyond them. The garrisons along the *limes* were systematically weakened by both these attacks and troop withdrawals to other areas of need. By A.D. 259-60, the barbarians had for the most part succeeded in pushing the Romans out of the frontier lands.[75]

Rome pushed back when Emperor Gallienus (A.D. 253-268) and his successors defeated the Franks and Alamanni and Aurelian (A.D. 270-275) defeated the Goths, thus securing the frontiers against major Germanic raids for another century. For some of the barbarians, defeat meant destruction of their social identity. The Roman army was often vicious in pursuing and destroying tribes and their villages and selling survivors into slavery. For warriors who surrendered, they were often sent in small groups throughout the empire and were assimilated into the Roman army. More common than total destruction was the reconstitution of the people in much the same form as before, but with certain obligations toward Rome as *foederati*. As such, they pledged they would defend

---

[75] Todd, *The Northern Barbarians* , 31-32; Gordon, "Subsidies in Roman Imperial Defence," 63, who remarked, "What Roman armies there were, were employed mostly in the service of pretenders to the supreme power rather than in the defence [sic] of the frontiers, and it was only diplomatic measures, including the widespread use of subsidization, that for long years preserved what little territorial integrity remained to the Empire… Indeed, all the northern tribes along the Rhine and Danube seem to have been more or less constantly bribed by the weak empire to keep the peace. These subsidies were not backed, however, by any reliable army and so led only to further demands and, when these were not promptly met, to invasion and devastation of all the northern provinces." This was especially true of the situation that led to the invasions of A.D. 406.

Rome's frontiers, provide troops when needed to the Roman army and, sometimes, to provide supplies.[76]

The third century saw the emergence of many new barbarian groups, "peoples" such as the Franks ("the Fierce" or "the Free") or the Alamanni ("the People"), neither of which could be traced to older, "ancient" peoples. Earlier, modern historians were wedded to theories of ethnological homogeneity and sought to discover and explain the origins of these groups as being splinters of larger groups mentioned by Tacitus. In fact, these were entirely new confederations of people located, in the case of the Franks, generally around the lower Rhine, and the Alamanni, generally around the upper Rhine. Beyond the Franks and Alamanni lay still other groups. The Burgundians and Saxons, neighbors to the Alamanni and the Franks, respectively, were probably new tribes who had assumed old names.[77] In the case of the Burgundians, it would be impossible to believe that all came from Bornholm and more likely that, in the most general sense, only the "nucleus" of this tribe, "the bearers of its traditions," had originally come from this place.[78]

Probus

The Burgundians moved westward sometime in the middle of the third century. They apparently took advantage of the chaos caused by the civil wars in the

---

[76] Geary, *The Myth of Nations*, 84.

[77] Ibid., 81.

[78] Musset, *Germanic Invasions*, 171.

Roman Empire following the murder of Maximinus in A.D. 238. Around A.D. 274, the Burgundians were among tribes that raided Gaul and sacked Trier and other towns. Writing in the fourth century, the historian Vopiscus mentioned an encounter between the Emperor Probus (A.D. 276-282) and a group of Germans near the Rhine. Zosimus, a Greek historian who wrote at the turn of the sixth century and relied upon earlier accounts, mentioned that the group of Germans attacked by Probus included both Burgundians and Vandals. Zosimus described that, in A.D. 277, Probus set out to reclaim Gaul from the Germans who had seized it. Though he had inferior numbers, Probus used a combination of taunting and tactics to prevail over his Germanic adversaries, killing many and driving the rest back over the Neckar River and beyond the Swabian Alb.[79]

Probus was not content merely to defeat them in a single battle, however, and he proceeded to strengthen the frontier along the Rhine to assist in making a more lasting impression upon the Germans. He built garrisoned camps on barbarian soil and provided supporting infrastructure, in the form of farms, houses, and storehouses.[80] He also provided rations of

---

[79] See Bernard S. Bachrach, "Burgundians," in *Dictionary of the Middle Ages*; Archeological evidence that has shown proof of the raids in Trier are mentioned in Anthony King, *Roman Gaul and Germany* (Berkeley: University of California Press, 1990), 176-7; Flavius Vopiscus, *Probus*, trans. David Magie in *The Scriptores Historiae Augustae*, vol.3, Loeb Classical Library (Cambridge, Mass.: Harvard University Press, 1932), 363-7; and Zosimus, *Historia Nova,* trans. James J. Buchanan and Harold T. Davis (San Antonio, TX: Trinity University Press, 1967), 41.

[80] H. Schonberger, "The Roman Frontier in Germany: An

grain for these troops beyond the Rhine. Thus strengthened, he continued to fight the barbarians and set a price for each head delivered to him. He only stopped when "nine princes of different tribes came before him and prostrated themselves at his feet."[81] Probus made a series of demands of these Germans, including a requirement that they supply him with hostages, grain, and livestock. He ordered them to lay down their swords because they would not need them as they were under the protection of Rome. With the consent of the barbarian princes, he severely punished those who had not given back booty.

Not all agreed to Probus's demands. Zosimus gave the name of a certain Igullus as being the leader of the Germans who refused to surrender their plunder, though whether he was a Burgundian or Vandal was not clear. According to Zosimus, Probus took Igullus and many recalcitrant Burgundians captive and shipped them

---

Archaeological Survey," *The Journal of Roman Studies* 59, no. ½ (1969): 178, noted that there is no archaeological proof supporting the claim that Probus established forts and settlements across the Rhine. However, "similar action must often have been taken before; any partial occupation of the right bank at this time, however, cannot have lasted long. It would fit the evidence well if the area between the Rhine, the Danube and the limes had formed a sort of no-man's land from 259-60 until about 300. It is then that the Germans first begin to leave tangible archaeological traces in this area."; also see Todd, *Everyday Life of The Barbarians*, 10, for the observation that archaeology has shown that the Celts and Germans were not so ethnically distinct as portrayed by Tacitus and Caesar and that the Rhine as a dividing line between the two cultures was not only misleading, but it obscured a third people who were neither definitively Celtic nor Germanic, though they were culturally similar.

[81] Vopiscus, *Probus*, 365.

to Britain where they settled and put down rebellions on Rome's behalf. Vopiscus confirmed that Probus took prisoners, and he also wrote that Probus took sixteen thousand recruits that he then dispersed throughout the provinces, placing small detachments of fifty or sixty among the soldiers along the reestablished frontier. [82]

Vopiscus asserted that Probus scattered these men in this surreptitious manner because he believed "that the aid that Romans received from barbarian auxiliaries must be felt but not seen."[83] Further, Vopiscus detailed a letter written by Probus and sent to members of the Roman senate in which Probus declared that "all of Germany . . . has now been subdued, and nine princes of different tribes have lain suplliant [sic] and prostrate at my feet, or, I should say, at yours . . . [the barbarians] plough for you, plant for you, and serve against the more distant tribes."[84]

The Accounts of Ammianus and Orosius

Under Diocletian (A.D. 284-305), the military was restructured, and two types of legions were created. The first, the *limitanei*, was composed of garrison troops along the heavily defended frontier and was composed mostly of ill-trained and ill-equipped local troops. The *comitatenses*, a mobile and more skilled field army, was rushed to assist these local border guards when emergency occurred. The *limitanei* gradually became

---

[82] Zosimus, *Historia Nova*, 41; and Vopiscus, *Probus,* 367.

[83] Vopiscus, *Probus,* 367.

[84] Ibid.

composed of local soldiers who were the sons of soldiers and the line between barbarian and Roman was blurred. The *comitatenses* also filled its ranks with barbarian recruits.[85]

Roughly eighty years after the Burgundian encounter with Probus, Ammianus Marcellinus wrote that, in A.D. 359, the Burgundian lands were located next to the Alamanni in a "region called Capillacii or Palas where boundary stones marked the frontiers of the Alamanni and Burgundians."[86] This placed the Burgundians somewhere east of the Alamanni, between the upper Rhine and Danube, possibly on the other side of the Roman *limes* that had been deserted in the third century.[87] Ammianus also wrote that the Burgundians knew that they were descendants of the Romans from ancient times and that he believed they had descended "from the Romans whom Drusus, and later Tiberius, left behind on the Elbe and elsewhere to defend the frontier."[88] That they did descend from Romans was possible given the aforementioned frontier garrison policies of Diocletian.

Paulus Orosius, writing around A.D. 417, also mentioned that the Burgundians were in this region

---

[85] Geary, *The Myth of Nations*, 89-92.

[86] Ammianus, *History*, 1:415.

[87] Heather, "The Huns," 14.

[88] Ammianus, *History*, 3:166-67; and Geary in *Before France and Germany*, 73, 75, points out that, although Ammianus' Burgundians may have formed in the fourth century, they maintained names and traditions linking them to ancient people of an earlier time and transferred this identity through various social formations.

along the Rhine during this period. According to Orosius, around the year A.D. 367, the Burgundians, "a new name for a new enemy" numbered 80,000 armed men who had settled on the Rhine.[89] Orosius generally confirmed Ammianus's theory of Burgundian descent, though this may indicate he used Ammianus as a source. Orosius added that these camps were in the interior of Germany and that the Germans had been dispersed to different camps, a possible reference to Vopiscus's account of Probus's policy towards the Burgundians. By A.D. 367, some of these people dispersed by Probus "came together to form a great nation and so even took their names from their work, because their frequent dwelling places" along the *limes* where they had settled and "assumed possession" were called "burgi."[90] As has been shown, it is possible that some unknown chief, perhaps with a legitimate ancestral claim to a Burgundian genealogy, had united these people.

In A.D. 369, the Emperor Valentinian I (A.D. 364-375) had recurring problems controlling the Alamanni and he asked for assistance from the Burgundians, "a warlike people, rich in a countless number of strong warriors, and therefore a cause of terror to all their

---

[89] Paulus Orosius, *The Seven Books of History Against the Pagans,* trans. Roy J. Deferrari, vol. 50, *The Fathers of the Church* (Washington, D.C.: Catholic University of America Press, 1964), 337; also see J.B. Bury, *History of the Later Roman Empire: From the Death of Theodosius I to the Death of Justinian* (New York: Dover Publications, Inc., 1958), 1:105. Bury noted Orosius' figure of 80,000 armed Burgundians along the Rhine, was probably more likely the total number of the Burgundian people at the beginning of the fifth century, when the account was written.

[90] Orosius, *History*, 337.

neighbours."[91] Valentinian sent secret letters that asked them to take part in a coordinated attack against the Alamanni. His plan called for the Burgundians to proceed with an initial attack and he and his Roman armies would support them by crossing the Rhine to prevent any Alamanni from escaping. Ammianus indicated that the Burgundians were amenable to these entreaties by the Emperor for two reasons. The first was because the Burgundians and Alamanni were traditional rivals. They frequently fought over important salt pits and the Burgundians saw this opportunity as a way to solidify their control of these valuable assets. The second reason ascribed by Ammianus was an alleged sense of kinship that the Burgundians felt toward the Romans, which recalled Ammianus' earlier assertions regarding the Burgundian heritage.[92]

The Burgundians sent their best warriors on the campaign and fought the Alamanni to the Rhine before the Romans had even put their forces in the field. The delay was caused by the Emperor's preoccupation with

---

[91] Ammianus, *History*, 3:165,167; also see Fredegar *Chron*. 2.46 (*MGH Script. Rer. Merov.*, vol 2, 68), in Goffart, *Barbarians and Romans*, 107. Writing in the seventh century, Fredegar said that, under Valentinian I, the Gallo-Romans invited the Burgundians so that they could stop paying taxes. Goffart points out that, while this could be the reason why the Burgundians were in the region at that time, the likelihood of Fredegar's claim was probably influenced more by contemporary, rather than historical, events.

[92] Wolfram, *Germanic Peoples*, 43, observed that Ammianus' feeling of closeness toward the Burgundians, owing to a shared *romanitas*, kept him from dismissing the unique Burgundian form of kingship as barbaric and instead elicited a comparison to the "sacral responsibility of Egyptian pharaohs."; and see note 91, page 43, below.

fortifying the frontier. This presumably distracted him from forming his army in time to support the Burgundians, as he had pledged. The sight of Burgundian war parties opposite the Rhine apparently caused fear among the Roman citizens. According to Ammianus, the Burgundians saw the panic they had caused and halted. They waited on the opposite shore for word from Valentinian.[93]

When neither Valentinian nor his forces appeared to be readying for war, the Burgundians believed, rightly, that he had reneged on his bargain. They decided to return to their homelands, but first sent envoys to him to demand that he, at the very least, protect their retreat against the Alamanni still in the region. Apparently, Valentinian refused to address these envoys "and when they perceived that by subterfuges and delays their request was practically denied, they went off from there in sorrow and indignation."[94] The Burgundian kings were informed by their envoys of Valentinian's disrespectful treatment and were greatly enraged. They proceeded to kill all of the Alamanni prisoners they had captured and returned to their lands.[95]

Ammianus also offered a description of the

---

[93] Ammianus, *History*, 3:167, 169.

[94] Ibid., 3:169.

[95] Ammianus, *History*, 3:169. Ammianus also mentioned that the Burgundians weakened the Alamanni to such an extent that, the following year, Theodosius, commander of the cavalry in Gaul, seeing that the Alamanni had scattered in fear of the Burgundians, attacked them, killed many and sent the prisoners to Italy.

Burgundian leadership:

> In their country a king is called by the general name Hendinos, and, according to an ancient custom, lays down his power and is deposed, if under him the fortune of war has wavered, or the earth has denied sufficient crops; just as the Egyptians commonly blame their rulers for such occurrences. On the other hand the chief priest among the Burgundians is called Sisistus, holds his power for life, and is exposed to no such dangers as threaten the kings.[96]

According to Ammianus, then, the dualistic Germanic leadership structure was in evidence among the Burgundians in the late fourth century. However, it seems that the *hendinos* was clearly in charge of military matters and seemed to have been held responsible for the general welfare of the tribe. The *sisistus* (also often called the *sinistus*) appeared to be a holy man who could probably trace his ancestry back to the tribe's founders.

---

[96] Ammianus, *History*, 3:169; and Ian Wood, "Kings, Kingdoms and Consent," in *Early Medieval Kingship*, eds. P.H. Sawyer and I.N. Wood (University of Leeds, 1977): 27, who noted that Ammianus Marcellinus' "famous description of sacral kingship among the Burgundians…demands cautious treatment. Ammianus compares the Burgundian system with that in use in Egypt. But Egypt did not have sacral kingship in the late fourth century A.D. This suggests that Ammianus is quoting a much earlier source. Whatever the source was, the evidence cannot be used at face value for a study of Burgundian kingship just before the migrations."

His position was more ceremonial. He had been a "king by noble birth" (*rex ex nobilitate*) and had been the leader of a smaller, essentially ethnically homogenous society. The *hendinos* had earned his position by his action and led a more diverse, and presumably larger, army.[97]

Those from the royal line of the *sisistus* were not necessarily excluded from becoming a *hendinos*. Should a line fail by being surpassed in deeds by one from another family, it was often the case that a new royal family, and often a tribe with new ethnic elements, would co-opt the ancient origin of an established people. This was probably how such tribal names as the Burgundians were kept alive. As the ancient tribal kingship model was replaced by the warrior king of migrating armies, the latter was forced to assume many of the political, or official, duties formally assigned to the *sisistus*. However, with greater power came greater responsibility, and the reverse, such that the *sisustus* was relatively secure in his position while the *hendinos* was often held directly accountable for the welfare of the tribe, regardless of his culpability.[98] Thus, it seems apparent that, according to Ammianus' observations, by this time the Burgundian *dux*, the *hendinos*, had gained the preeminent position of authority among the Burgundians.

---

[97] Wolfram, *Germanic Peoples*, 18.
[98] Ibid.

CHAPTER 3
THE FIRST BURGUNDIAN KINGDOM
(C.400 A.D. TO 436 A.D.)

Constantine and Jovinus

As the empire grew, Rome demanded the provincial landowners pay higher municipal assessments. These landowners passed as much of this burden as they could onto the tenant farmers and slaves on their lands, who, with no other recourse, would sometimes revolt against their landowners. Thus, brigandage (armed rebellion) spread, and the landowners, now often without sufficient workers on their lands, were still required to pay the assessments, regardless of their own ability to collect taxes. They viewed Rome as a greater threat than barbarian incursion and, when faced with the inability of the former to deal adequately with the latter, resorted to raising their own commanders to deal with the problems of rebellion and barbarian raids. When these champions were successful, they would further be raised as emperors, as in the case of Cassius Latinus Postumus and his Gallic Empire from A.D. 259 to A.D. 273.[99]

These events foreshadowed a growing attitude among the provincial Romans. They were more concerned with their immediate welfare than with maintaining a remote ideal of a united Roman empire and, when faced with chaos, turned to whomever could provide immediate relief. Self-interest won out over idealism.[100]

In the fifth century this attitude became the norm. On December 31, 406, Vandals and Alans crossed the Rhine and entered Gaul to raid, pillage and burn. Shortly thereafter, about A.D. 407, the Burgundians filled the vacuum created by the departure of the Vandals and moved down the Main River and ravaged Strassburg, Speier and Worms in the process. They fought and pushed out the Alamanni and occupied new territory on both sides of the Rhine by A.D. 411. Traditionally, their establishment in this region has been called the Kingdom of Worms, apparently in an attempt to align history with the tales of the *Nibelungenlied*. In fact, the kingdom is thought to have been located on the Rhine, downstream of Koblenz, in Germania II rather than Germania I. As a result of this historiographical argument, some scholars began referring to it as the Rhenish kingdom of the Burgundians.[101]

---

[99] Geary, *The Myth of Nations*, 79-80.

[100] Ibid., 80-81.

[101] Mathisen, *Roman Aristocrats*, 39-41, explained that Ausonius, Jerome in A.D. 406, Nazarius in the early fourth century, Sidonius in the fifth century (twice), and Avitus of Vienne in the 6th century all gave approximately the same list of barbarian tribes who they said invaded the

During this time, the Roman imperial claimant Constantine III (A.D. 409-411) had entered the Rhône valley. He encountered certain barbarian tribes, which are believed to have been Burgundians and Alamanni. At that time, Constantine made some sort of mutually beneficial agreement with these tribes, which they later violated. Further, it seems both groups, the barbarians and Constantine, continued to operate independently of each other in the region, in a sort of acquiescence of feigned ignorance.[102] It seems apparent that if the Burgundians did indeed drive the Alamanni out of territory they occupied, then the two groups may also have had a falling out.

After Constantine III was killed, Jovinus (A.D. 411-

---

empire. These lists indicated no uniquely identifying quality for any of these groups and the frequent mention of the same list seems to indicate that it was a standard litany used to illustrate that there were barbarians invading the empire; *Prosperi Tironis epitoma chronicon*, ed. Th. Mommsen, *Chronica Minora I, MGH AA 9* (1892), 385-485. trans. A.C. Murray, in *From Roman to Merovingian Gaul: A Reader,* ed. and trans. Alexander Callander Murray (Orchard Park, NY: Broadview Press, 2000), 64; L. Schmidt, *Geschichte der Wandalen*, 1901, in Bury, *Roman Empire*, 1:187; Peter Heather, "The Huns," 14; Robert Latouche, "Agriculture in the Early Middle Ages," in *The Barbarian Invasions: Catalyst of a New Order*, ed. Katherine Fischer Drew (New York: Holt, Rinehart and Winston, 1970), 90, for the Greek historian Socrates' assertion that the Burgundians crossed the Rhine to pursue their primary trade of carpentry and woodworking. This seems a curious passage, though it may have a grain of truth. Perhaps the Burgundians were known for their woodworking talents, though no other evidence to support this can be found in the sources; Musset, *Germanic Invasions*, 62, for the argument that a more accurate placement of the first Burgundian kingdom is near Koblenz.

[102] Orosius, *Historiae adv. Paganos*, edited by Zangemeister (1889) and E.A. Freeman, *Western Europe in the Fifth Century* (1904) in Bury, *Roman Empire*, 1:189.

412), a Gallo-Roman in northern Gaul, was raised as emperor with the support of the Burgundians. It has also been suggested that Roman officials who had previously supported Constantine III also supported Jovinus. This support of Jovinus for Emperor by the Burgundians was an attempt to strengthen their position within the wider Roman Empire. However, the reign of Jovinus was brief, and the Burgundian's role as imperial power brokers proved a temporary one. Athaulf and his Visigoths eventually killed Jovinus at the behest of Rome in A.D. 413. [103]

After the fall of Jovinus, Prosper of Aquitaine wrote that the Burgundians "acquired part of Gaul near the Rhine."[104]   Prior to their support of Jovinus,

---

[103] *Chronica Gallica A. CCCCLII*, ed. Th. Mommsen, *Chronica Minor I, MGH AA 9* (1892), 646-62, trans. by A.C. Murray, in Murray, *Merovingian Gaul,* 81. (hereafter cited as *Chronicle of 452*); *Prosperi Tironis,* in Murray, *Merovingian Gaul,* 64; Gregory of Tours, *The History of the Franks,* trans. with an introduction by Lewis Thorpe (London: Penguin Books, 1974), 124-25; Mathisen, *Roman Aristocrats,* 82; see Heather, "The Huns" (20-21) in which it is explained that it was common practice for barbarian groups to attempt to strengthen their position within the Empire by supporting rebellion when the opportunity arose, rather than by attempting to set up an independent state, by directly usurping land from the Roman Empire; this is supported by Ralph W. Mathisen, "Proculus, Patroclus, and Pelagianism: The Gallic Church in the Age of the Tyrants," in *Ecclesiastical Factionalism and Religious Controversy in Fifth-Century Gaul*, (Washington, D.C.: The Catholic University Press, 1989), 27-43, which described how both Roman political and ecclesiastical factions were just as, if not more, involved in the rise and fall of the various "tyrannical" emperors as were the barbarian groups and their kings; and *The Chronicle of Hydatius and the Consularia Constantinopolitana*, ed. and trans. Richard W. Burgess (Oxford, 1993), trans. A.C. Murray, in Murray, *Merovingian Gaul,* 87.

[104] *Prosperi Tironis*, in Murray, *Merovingian Gaul,* 65.

Constantine III had confirmed the Burgundians in their possession of the land they had seized along the Rhine. The new emperor, Honorius, accepted them as Federates of the Empire (*foederati*), probably more out of necessity than desire. As such, in A.D. 413, they were established along the Rhine and pledged to guard the empire against its enemies. This was the first Burgundian kingdom in Gaul, under their king, Gundahar. [105]

The Conversion of the Burgundians

By A.D. 417, the historian Orosius wrote, the Burgundians, a "strong and destructive nation," had accepted the Catholic faith and "live kindly, gentle, and harmless lives, not, as it were, with the Gauls as their subjects, but really as their Christian brothers."[106] Additionally, Orosius wrote that:

> The barbarians, detesting their swords, turned to their ploughs and now cherish the Romans as comrades and friends, so that now there may be found among them certain Romans who prefer poverty with freedom among the barbarians than paying tribute with anxiety among the Romans . . . throughout the East and the West the churches of Christ were replete with Huns, Suevi, Vandals, and

---

[105] Bury, *Roman Empire*, 200.
[106] Orosius, *Seven Books of History,* 337.

53

Burgundians.[107]

Despite Orosius's contention, it is not known exactly when or how the Burgundians converted to Christianity.[108] Barbarian warriors serving in the Roman army may have brought Christianity back to their tribes with them. However, unless the individual was a chief, he was probably unable to persuade many of his tribesmen to follow his new religion. He also risked being marked as an outcast for embracing a foreign god. The Christian hostages held by the barbarians were probably the most influential force in their conversion. More knowledgeable in the healing arts than their captors, these Christians wielded this curative sword of healing, upheld by the strength of their Catholic faith, and conquered their captors for the church.[109]

---

[107] Orosius, *Seven Books of History*, 358; However, also see E.A. Thompson, "Christianity and the Northern Barbarians," in *The Conflict Between Paganism and Christianity in the Fourth Century*, ed. Arnaldo Momigliano (London: Oxford University Press, 1963), 71, 76-77, for the assertion that Orosius' statement that the Burgundians were converted to Catholicism by A.D. 417 "is generally discounted and may be dismissed" and that, no matter how the Germans were converted, the actions of Roman missionaries played only a very small part. Thompson concluded that, although many Catholic bishops worked among the Germans when they entered the Empire as *foederati*, they were not converted at this time.

[108] To clarify, I have attempted to use the terms "Catholic" to explicitly mean Orthodox Christianity or Roman Catholicism, "Arian" to explicitly mean heretical Arian Christianity, and "Christianity" as a more general term. For a discussion of the difference between Roman Catholicism and Arianism, see page 60.

[109] Thompson, "Christianity and the Northern Barbarians," 56-58; and see Paul Lacroix, *Science and Literature in the Middle Ages and the Renaissance* (New York: Frederick Unger Publishing Co., 1878), 136-137,

Another way that Christianity entered the barbarian world was through commerce and trade. Missionaries traveled the trade routes where they often persuaded local chieftains, usually with a few gifts, to allow them to preach in the village without repercussions against either themselves or any new barbarian converts. The most successful would secure permission to build a church and thus help to ensure that the barbarians would continue to be exposed to Christianity. Often, these missionaries were supported by not only the Church, but also the emperor who saw political opportunity in religious conversion.[110] Yet, these instances were scattered and uncommon. The first serious, or at least well-documented, attempt at proselytizing amongst the Germans did not occur until the middle of the fourth century, when Ulfilas was sent to preach in the Goth lands.

Ulfilas, though descended from a Cappadocian family, had been raised a Goth and sent as a youth to Constantinople as a hostage. In Constantinople he converted to Arian Christianity, was consecrated a bishop at the age of thirty (A.D. 341) and was sent by Eusebius of Nicomedia to proselytize and spread Arian Christianity among the Goths.[111] Eventually, Ulfilas was

---

who explained that by the end of the fourth century, it was common for Christian churches and monasteries to open their doors to the sick. The first leper houses were usually built near churches. As such, there was an association between Christians and healing, who saw to "[t]he wants both of the body and soul."

[110] Ibid., 58-59.

[111] See Bury, *Invasion of Europe*, 45, for the position that Ulfilas was

forced to leave the Goth lands because of persecution from Goth leaders. However, only some of the Arian Christian Goths followed him to new lands in Moesia, within the borders of the Roman Empire. Other Arian Goths refused to leave and, despite persecution and martyrdom, Arian Christianity gained a foothold among the Goths. Eventually, the other Germanic tribes, including the Burgundians, converted to Arianism.[112]

Ulfilas is best known for both inventing the Goth alphabet and translating the Bible into Gothic. Equally important was that he was not a Catholic but followed the Arian heresy developed by the bishop Arius of Alexandria in the fourth century. Arians held that neither Jesus nor the Holy Spirit were co-equal with God. Additionally, Jesus had been created by God and was not eternal. This was contrary to the Catholic position that Christ was 'fully God, fully man,' that He had always existed and always would and that he had assumed human form to instruct and to suffer and die for humanity.[113]

---

sent to preach Arian Christianity to all in the Goth lands. An alternative view was put forth by Thompson, "Christianity and the Northern Barbarians," 64, who asserted that Ulfilas was sent to minister only to those Christians already in the Goth lands, such as Roman prisoners or their descendents, and not to convert pagan Goths. As such, Thompson continued, "[T]he Churches of the fourth and fifth centuries delayed for a curiously long time to send bishops to their captive sons and daughters beyond the frontier; and they made little or no organized or planned effort to save the barbarians from the fire everlasting."

[112] Bury, *Invasion of Europe*, 44-47.

[113] See C. Warren Hollister, *Medieval Europe: A Short History*, 8th ed. (New York: McGraw-Hill, 1998), 19-20; and Roger Collins, *Early Medieval Europe, 300-1000*, 2d ed. (New York: Palgrave, 1999), 64.

The Roman Emperor Constantine called the First Council of Nicea in A.D. 325 in an attempt to resolve the conflict and Arianism was condemned, though only temporarily. Under the reign of the Arian Emperor Constantius II Arianism became ascendant though his successor, the pagan emperor Julian, encouraged conflict between Catholics and Arians. The ascension of Valens in A.D. 364 returned Arianism to preeminence in the eyes of the empire and it was during his reign that Ulfilas journeyed to the Goth lands and planted the seeds of Arianism. In A.D. 379, the Catholic Theodosius I assumed the reign of the East and he called the First Council of Constantinople in A.D. 381 at which Arianism was outlawed throughout the Roman Empire. Outside it, however, Arianism had taken hold amongst the Germanic tribes, over whom Rome held no power to dictate religious preferences.[114]

Ammianus gave no hint that the Burgundians had abandoned their pagan religion or priesthood when he wrote his history circa A.D. 395, so it must be assumed that they were still pagan upon entering Gaul in A.D. 406. Despite Orosius' contention that the Burgundians were Catholic by A.D. 417, it seems improbable that a Catholic missionary would have journeyed through Germany and bypassed other tribes to specifically preach to the Burgundians. Additionally, the Gallic Chronicle implies that all of the major Germanic tribes

---

[114] Hollister, *Medieval Europe*, 20-22; and Collins, *Early Medieval Europe,* 64-65.

were Arian by A.D. 451.[115]

Most historians have come to believe that the Burgundians actually converted to Arianism sometime prior to A.D. 436,[116] probably when they were settled as *foederati* in Germania I. This would justify the story told by the historian Socrates that the eastern Burgundians, those who had stayed on the eastern shore of the Rhine when most of their brethren crossed over into Gaul in A.D. 406, had become Christian around A.D. 430. Although the relationship between the two branches of Burgundians remains unknown, it is probably safe to assume that both groups were converted at about the same time.[117]

The question of who converted the Burgundians remains a mystery. Some have theorized that a pocket of Roman Arians along the Rhine converted the Burgundians. Yet, it is more likely that a group of Visigothic missionaries preached to and converted the Burgundians some time after A.D. 418. Since any such

---

[115] Thompson, "Christianity and the Northern Barbarians," 71; *Chronicle of 452*, 85; but also see Otto Maenchen-Helfen, *The World of the Huns*, (Berkeley: University of California Press, 1973): 82 f. in Wolfram, *Germanic Peoples*, 258, where it is stated that "The Burgundians on the right bank of the Rhine supposedly all turned Catholic to successfully fend off the Hunnic threat."

[116] Musset, *Germanic Invasions*, 63.

[117] Socrates, 7.30.3, *Chronica Minora*, ii. 491, in Thompson, "Christianity and the Northern Barbarians," 72; and James C. Russell, *The Germanization of Early Medieval Christianity: A Sociohistorical Approach to Religious Transformation* (New York: Oxford University Press, 1994), 138, for the theory that "[a] political alliance of the Burgundians with the Visigoths against the Huns in 451 may have contributed to sympathy among Burgundians for Arianism."

mission at this time would have had to deal with the Huns, any belief that a large group of Visigothic missionaries went traipsing about the Rhine, surrounded by Huns, is probably an exaggeration.[118] This does not exclude the possibility that a smaller group of Visigothic missionaries could have performed the task.

Most of the conversions were more likely the result of a slow, religious osmosis. By settling in Roman lands, surrounded by Romans, Germans were exposed to Christianity. Nonetheless, a people that linked riches, success and the like to their religion could not help but recognize the benefit of praying to the god of their prosperous neighbors.[119] "The move into a new economic and social world was necessarily followed by a move into a new spiritual world."[120] Thus the Burgundians adopted Arian Christianity and prayed to the Christian God from whom they expected to reap the benefit.

That the majority of the Germanic tribes followed heretical Arianism was probably not an accident. As it had fallen out of favor within the empire, it had increased its influence among the Germanic people outside of the empire. In the case of the Visigoths under

---

[118] Thompson, "Christianity and the Northern Barbarians," 77.

[119] Russell, *The Germanization of Early Medieval Christianity*, 135-36, showed that, from the beginning, in A.D. 376, when the Goths negotiated with the Arian Christian Emperor of the Eastern Empire Valens to enter imperial lands, religion was used as a political tool. It was a way "in which political leaders vouched for their subjects" and it also showed that Roman culture was associated with Christianity. One could not be Roman and not be a Christian.

[120] Thompson, "Christianity and the Northern Barbarians," 78.

Theodosius, the barbarians preferred the decentralized, mostly locally governed church of Arian Christianity over the organized and centrally governed Catholic faith, which they believed would intrude upon their traditions and tend to weaken their social identity. The same attitude has been ascribed to the Burgundians.[121] By adhering to what was regarded as a heretical form of Christianity, the already outnumbered Burgundians only increased their isolation amidst a sea of Gallo-Roman Christians.[122]

Any bonds, be they genealogical or religious, that the Burgundians felt with their Gallo-Roman neighbors were not strong enough to prevent the Gallo-Romans from complaining of Burgundian territorial encroachment. By about A.D. 435, the Burgundians had made many attempts to expand their kingdom by invading the province of Upper Belgica, apparently in the belief that Rome had either weakened or was distracted elsewhere.[123] It was unfortunate for them that at the

---

[121] E.A. Thompson, *The Visigoths in the Time of Ulfila* (Oxford: Clarendon Press, 1966), 110, in Russell, *The Germanization of Early Medieval Christianity*, 139-40.

[122] Pierre Riche, *Education and Culture in the Barbarian West: From the Sixth Through the Eighth Century*, trans. John J. Contreni, with a foreword by Richard E. Sullivan (Columbia: University of South Carolina Press, 1976), 218-19, in Russell, *The Germanization of Early Medieval Christianity*, 143-44. Russell, relying on Riche, wrote, "Barbarian and Gothic aristocrats imitated the Roman way of life, but as we have seen, they were not won over to classical culture. Their own culture and the Arian religion they professed help to explain their indifference." This seems too dismissive of the willingness of the various Germanic tribes to embrace Roman culture.

[123] E.A. Thompson, *A History of Attila and the Huns* (London: Oxford

time the Roman general in Gaul was Aëtius, an extremely capable man.

The Rise of Aëtius

After the fall of Stilicho in A.D. 408, the Roman empire had decided to secure military assistance from a non-Germanic source and made a treaty with the Huns, which included the exchange of hostages. One of these was a young Roman named Aëtius.[124] By A.D. 425 he had been freed, but his familiarity with the Huns prompted the usurper John, who was in desperate need of military help to ward off an attack at Ravenna, to send Aëtius to the Huns with the objective of hiring an army. Unfortunately for John, Aëtius arrived too late to save him, but Aëtius was later successful in persuading the Huns to leave Italy in return for booty and hostages. As a result of this remarkable diplomacy, Placidia and Valentinian III forgave him for fighting against them and gave him an imperial title.[125]

In A.D. 432, Aëtius lost to his rival Boniface of Africa in a battle fought near Ariminum. Though he returned to his estate, he maintained enough military strength to preclude an open attack from his enemies. However, Boniface's son-in-law, Sebastian, attempted to have Aëtius assassinated. The failed attempt on his life prompted Aëtius to leave his estates and he eventually

University Press, 1948; reprint, Westport, Conn.: Greenwood Press, 1975), 65 (page citations are to the reprint edition); and Musset, *Germanic Invasions*, 184.

[124] Thompson, *A History of Attila and the Huns*, 33.

[125] Ibid., 35.

found his way to the Huns, ruled at that time by Rua. Aëtius made a treaty with the Huns in which he handed over Pannonia Prima and also sent his own son, Carpilio, as a hostage. With his new Hun allies, Aëtius secured his own position in the Empire and faced down Sebastian, becoming a patrician. He would turn repeatedly to his Hun allies to assist him in protecting Gallo-Roman interests.[126]

The Destruction of the First Burgundian Kingdom

The Burgundians were one of the first Germanic tribes against whom Aëtius marched, with the goal of preventing their further encroachment on Roman soil. Hydatius wrote, "The Burgundians, who had rebelled, were defeated by the Romans under the general Aëtius."[127] According to Prosper of Aquitaine, "Aëtius crushed [Gundahar], who was king of the Burgundians and living in Gaul. In response to his entreaty, Aëtius gave him peace, which the king did not enjoy for long. For the Huns destroyed him and his people root and branch."[128] Various other chronicles put the date of these events in the same approximate time frame, and all lay the defeat of the Burgundians at the feet of Aëtius and the Huns.[129]

---

[126] Ibid., 63-4.

[127] *Hydatius*, in Murray, *Merovingian Gaul*, 89.

[128] *Prosperi Tironis*, in Murray, *Merovingian Gaul*, 69.

[129] *Hydatius*, in Murray, *Merovingian Gaul*, 89; and *Chronicle of 452*, in Murray, *Merovingian Gaul*, 83; and see Walter Goffart, "Rome, Constantinople, and the Barbarians," *The American Historical Review* 86, no.2 (1981): 295. Aëtius often pitted barbarians against each other for the

That Aëtius and the Huns both attacked the Burgundians has not been disputed. Whether the Huns proceeded with their attack at the bidding of the Roman general, or did so for other reasons, remains unknown. A comparison of the accounts given in the chronicles only adds to the confusion. Hydatius credited Aëtius, or forces under his command, for defeating the Burgundians in both A.D. 436 and A.D. 437, while another anonymous chronicler only mentioned that Aëtius was responsible defeating the Burgundians in A.D. 436 and made no mention of a second confrontation.[130] Yet, it is the aforementioned account of Prosper of Aquitaine, who lived during the time of the events, which may provide a hint as to what really occurred.

Prosper clearly separated the two attacks upon the Burgundians as well as those responsible. This does not exclude the possibility that the Huns were acting on behalf of Aëtius. If true, then it seems likely that Aëtius broke his peace with the Burgundians and their spectacular defeat could have resulted from a mistaken belief that they were at peace. In short, they weren't prepared for war, especially in a weakened state. However, another interpretation of Prosper's account

---

benefit of Rome. This policy was common, as Roman Emperors were reticent to rely on Roman armies because of a fear of civil war. Imperial authorities had long forbidden men of senatorial rank from joining the army and relied upon the populace in the cities to keep the economy moving. As a result, most of the city and country population of the Roman Empire had nothing to do with the military and the best, and only, recruits left were the barbarians.

[130] *Hydatius*, in Murray, *Merovingian Gaul*, 89; and *Chronicle of 452*, in Murray, *Merovingian Gaul*, 83.

would indicate that the two separate attacks were committed by different forces and implies differing motivations on the part of each aggressor.[131] Aëtius' motivation was clear. He sought to protect the Gallic aristocracy from Burgundian encroachment. The reasons behind a Hunnic attack are more difficult to determine.

It has been suggested that the Huns may have had their own reasons for attacking the Burgundians. Some contemporary writers wrote that a portion of the Burgundians had not crossed the Rhine with the bulk of their people. Instead, they remained on the eastern shore of the Rhine, in the region between it, the Main, and the Neckar rivers. According to the ecclesiastical historian Socrates, around A.D. 430, these Burgundians were suffering continuous attacks by the Huns, with devastating results. Apparently, they spurned their traditional, but ineffective, gods and turned to the Christian god for help. According to the story, their prayers were answered when Uptar, the king of this branch of the Huns, exploded, and subsequently died, as a result of a night of overindulgence. His leaderless tribe of 10,000 was then easily defeated by a force of only 3,000 Burgundians. Finally, because of this stunning victory, the Burgundians became devout Christians.[132]

---

[131] Norman H. Baynes, "A Note on Professor Bury's 'History of the Later Roman Empire'," *The Journal of Roman Studies* 12 (1922): 221.

[132] *Socrates*, vii, 30, in Thompson, *A History of Attila and the Huns*, 66; and see Socrates Scholasticus, *The Ecclesiastical History of Socrates Scholasticus*, in *Socrates and Sozomenus: Ecclesiastical Histories,* rev. A.C. Zenos, A Select library of Nicene and post-Nicene fathers of the Christian

While this is undoubtedly a conversion story, some details are verified in other sources. Uptar is probably the same person as Octar, the brother of Rua, king of the Huns, who assisted Aëtius. Additionally, the relatively small number of warriors engaged in the battle was notable given that the account was written by an ecclesiastical historian, clerics usually given to inflating the size of medieval military forces. Given this, it can be theorized that a group of Huns, led by the brother of Rua, regularly ravaged the Burgundians but were eventually, and unexpectedly, defeated by their one-time victims. As such, the acts later attributed to the Huns, whether singly or at the behest of Aëtius, may have been the result of a desire for revenge.[133] However, and perhaps more simply, it could also be a case of a strong Hun army attacking a weak neighbor for booty and treasure. They would not have needed the blessing, or prompting, of Aëtius to embark on such a campaign.

Regardless of their motivation, the Huns were effective in reducing the Burgundians "to manageable dimensions, the manner in which this was done becoming a main theme of bardic recitation."[134] It was

---

church : Second series, ed. and trans. Philip Schaff and Henry Wace, vol. 2, (New York: The Christian Literature Company, 1890), 169-170, and see ibid., 279-280, regarding the death of the Arian heretic Arius for another example of this kind of expiration. Taking Socrates' examples, it seems prayers were often answered with explosive results.

[133] Thompson, *A History of Attila and the Huns*, 66-67.

[134] J.M. Wallace-Hadrill, *The Barbarian West, 400-1000* (Oxford: Blackwell Publishers Inc., 1999), 27-28.

such a remarkable event that it was mentioned by several of the extant chroniclers.[135] This "bardic recitation" eventually became known as the *Nibelungenlied*. The encounter with the Huns may not have only inspired an epic tale. According to some, it was shortly after this time that the Burgundians began to emulate the look of their conquerors as they copied Hunnic fashion and even practiced cranial deformation.[136]

---

[135] Thompson, *A History of Attila and the Huns*, 65; however, as mentioned previously, see *Hydatius*, in Murray, *Merovingian Gaul*, 89, and the *Chronicle of 452*, in Murray, *Merovingian Gaul*, 83, neither of which explicitly mentioned that the Huns were involved. For mention of the Huns, see *Prosperi Tironis*, in Murray, *Merovingian Gaul*, 69, but it only explicitly stated that the Huns acted after, and perhaps independently of, Aëtius. As such, the fall of the Burgundians may have inspired legend, but whether the Huns caused their downfall remains a subject for debate.

[136] Musset, *Germanic Invasions*, 21,31.

CHAPTER 4
GERMANIC MYTH AND THE BURGUNDIANS

Early in the thirteenth century, circa A.D. 1200, an anonymous scribe somewhere along the Danube wrote down the old stories, based on even older Germanic myths, that became known as the *Nibelungenlied*. This tale was supposedly based on the events surrounding the collapse of the kingdom of the Burgundians around A.D. 436/7 and, in particular, it told of the spectacular fall of the royal family at the time, the Gibichungs.[137] The king of the Burgundians at the time of the tale was Gundahar (Gunther). He was the first historical Burgundian king mentioned, though a tribal history outlined in the *Lex Burgundionum* of a hundred years later said he was but the fourth king of the line of Gibichungs, founded by Gibica.[138] The *Nibelungenlied* was based on older Germanic tales, which survive in the Eddas and the Volsung saga. In turn, these stories were derived from an even earlier mythical tradition. Though

---

[137] Wolfram, *Germanic Peoples*, 248; and see "Nibelungenlied," in *Dictionary of the Middle Ages*, Joseph Strayer, ed., (New York: Charles Scribner's Sons, 1987), 9: 112-115, for a good summary.
[138] Ibid., 250.

not necessarily "historic," the tales are still instructive and supply some clues as to how myth intertwined with actual historical fact or accepted historical belief.

Slagfinn

According to these legends, Ivalde was the only being, mortal or god, who knew the source from whence the purest form of the drink, called *soma*, came. *Soma* gave the gods in Asgard, led by Odin, their power and wisdom. The gods partook of a less pure form, but strove to learn of Ivalde's secret. Ivalde had had three sons, Slagfinn, Egil, and Völund, born to him by Greip, a giantess. One night, Ivalde sent his son Slagfinn and a daughter, Bil, to get a flask of *soma* for him. After collecting the mead, they were kidnapped by the Moon God, who then dispensed the *soma* to the other gods of Asgard. Angered, Ivalde kidnapped the Moon God's daughter, apparently a sort of Sun demi-Goddess, and she eventually bore him many daughters, all of whom were associated with growth and rejuvenation. A feud between Ivalde and the Moon God erupted.[139]

However, though their father was at war with the gods, Ivalde's sons, especially Slagfinn, maintained their friendship with the denizens of Asgard. In Slagfinn's case, he became particularly close to his now foster-father, the moon-god. From this relationship,

---

[139] Viktor Rydberg, *Teutonic Mythology: Gods And Goddesses Of The Northland*, trans. Rasmus B. Anderson, Memorial Edition, 3 vols., Norrœna Anglo-Saxon classics, vols. 3-5, (London: Norrœna Society, 1907): 3:1002-1004.

Slagfinn thereafter also became known as Huki or Gjuki.[140] Ivalde was defeated in his war with the gods and agreed to an oath of peace. However, this did not last for long. Ivalde later broke the treaty and was defeated and killed.[141]

After the death of their father Slagfinn- Gjuki[142] and his brothers Volund and Egil, who were excellent smiths, maintained their friendship with the gods in Asgard for a time, making many treasures for them. However, they too eventually sought to topple the gods. Their attempt failed. Defeated, they departed their lands, running on skis, toward the northern reaches of the world and arrived in the Wolf-dales. There, they met the swan maids, demi-goddesses of growth (and probably their half-sisters), who joined them in their plotting against the gods.[143] Eventually, however, the swan-maids decided to return south and made their escape while the brothers were away hunting. Upon discovering that their companions had left, Slagfinn-Gjuki and Egil, this time wearing snowshoes, went in

---

[140] Rydberg, *Teutonic Mythology*, 3:1006.

[141] Ibid., 3:999-1000.

[142] Rydberg, *Teutonic Mythology*, 3: 991, concluded from his research that. "[t]he names by which Slagfinn is found in our records are accordingly Iði, Gjúki, Dankrat (Þakkráður), Irung, Aldrian, Cheldricus, Gelderus, Hjúki…[and] Hengest (Hengist)….The most important Slagfinn epithets, from a mythological standpoint, are Idi, Gjuki, Hjuki, and Irung." Also see (3:988-89) for the determination that Slagfinn and his brothers are Niflungs and that he was also adopted by the moon-god, "whose name he bore. Gjuki and Hjuki are therefore names borne by one and the same person - by Slagfinn, the Niflung."

[143] Rydberg, *Teutonic Mythology*, 3:917-18.

search of their swan-maids while Volund stayed behind. Slagfinn-Gjuki searched for his swan-maid, Svanhvít, to the south, while Egil sought his to the east.[144]

Slagfinn-Gjuki eventually found his way to his father's old hall and claimed the hall and the treasure within as his inheritance. Whether this was equal to his one-third share of the total treasure of Ivalde or if it was the entire fortune is not clear, but he shared it with his two brothers. Slagfinn-Gjuki buried his portion of the treasure inside a mountain for safekeeping. It was the quest for this mythical treasure, the *Nibelunge Hort*, which inspired many of the Germanic tales. It was from Slagfinn-Gjuki that the Gjukungs were said to have sprung, making the Gjukungs one line of the Niflung, or Nibelung, race, and thus rightful heirs to the treasure.[145] Eventually, most of the treasure was collected by the Gjukungs, thanks to their own efforts and those of the mythic hero, Sigurd.[146]

The Gjukungs

Seeking adventure, Sigurd had traveled from his home and come upon a princess, Brynhild, daughter of King Budli, in her castle. They fell in love, and Sigurd

---

[144] Rydberg, *Teutonic Mythology*, 3:971, 982; and *The Elder Edda of Saemund Sigfusson*., trans. Benjamin Thorpe and *The Younger Edda of Snorre Sturleson*, trans. I.A. Blackwell, ed. Rasmus B. Anderson, (London: Norrœna Society, 1907): 121.

[145] Rydberg, *Teutonic Mythology*, 3:974-75, 972-73, and (3:981-85) for the explanation that another of Slagfinn-Gjuki's many names was Gibich. Thus, sometimes the Nibelungs are referred to as the Gibechungs.

[146] Ibid., 3:975-76.

gave her a ring before leaving for further adventure. He rode to the lands of King Gjuki, who was married to Grimhild the Wise. They had three sons, Gunnar, Hogni, Guony, and a daughter, Gudrun, as well as a stepson, Gotthorm. Sigurd enjoyed his stay with this family and befriended the sons of Gjuki. Sigurd's friendship with Gunnar and Hogni grew especially deep and the three warriors pledged mutual bonds of brotherhood. Sigurd formed an even stronger bond with their sister, Gudrun, whom he married and by whom he had two children, Sigmund and Svanhild.[147]

One day, Sigurd and the sons of Gjuki went to King Atli, son of Budli and brother to Brynhild, on behalf of Gunnar to ask for Brynhild's hand in marriage. Brynhild lived in a hall called Hinafjall, surrounded by a wall of flame and had sworn that she would only marry the man who could ride through the flames. She had demanded this because she believed that only Sigurd, her true love, would be able to accomplish such a task. Gunnar was not swayed and strove to make the attempt, but his horse did not dare to jump through the flames. Sigurd's horse was the only one that would brave the flames, but the horse only allowed Sigurd to seat him. Thus, Sigurd and Gunnar "changed shapes and also names" and in the guise of Sigurd, Gunnar won the hand of Brynhild and all returned to the lands of Gjuki.[148]

---

[147] *The Prose Edda of Snorri Sturluson: Tales from Norse Mythology*, with an introduction by Sigurdur Nordal, trans. Jean I. Young (Berkeley: University of California Press, 1966), 113-14.

[148] Ibid., 114.

Eventually, the ruse played upon Brynhild was revealed to her by Gudrun. Full of vengeance, she urged her husband Gunnar and brother-in-law Hogni to kill Sigurd. However, they had sworn an oath as brothers to Sigurd and contrived to have their step-brother Gotthorm commit the act. Gotthorm succeeded in killing both Sigurd and his three year old son Sigmund, but was himself killed in the act. Gunnar and Hogni took Sigurd's treasure for themselves and ruled the land. Brynhild committed suicide.[149] No fairy tale, this!

Atli married Sigurd's widow Gudrun and invited his new brother-in-laws Gunnar and Hogni to his home. Before their journey, they buried their treasure in the Rhine and then went to Atli's home where they were attacked and taken prisoner. Atli cut out Hogni's heart and threw Gunnar in a snake pit. "A harp was procured for him in secret and, because his hands were tied, he played it with his toes in such a way that all the snakes went to sleep, but for one adder, which made for him and gnawing its way through the cartilage of his breast-bone thrust its head through the hole and buried its fangs in his liver until he was dead."[150] The sons of Gjuki, the Gjukungs or Nibelungs, were no more, and their treasure, the inheritance of the Nibelungs, was lost.

Gudrun, with the help of Hogni's son had her revenge on Atli, drugging his mead and killing him while he was in a stupor. Then she burned his hall with all of his people within. After that, she tried to drown herself

---

[149] Ibid., 114-15.
[150] Ibid., 115.

in the sea but drifted and came to the land of King Jonak, whom she married and by whom she had three sons. Her daughter Svanhild eventually joined her in this new land. Svanhild grew up to be a beautiful woman and was the object of jealousy between King Jormunrekk and his son Randver. The result of the jealous conflict was the death of both Randver and Svanhild at the hands of the old king. Gudrun urged her sons to avenge the death of their half-sister, which they did. However, the three sons also perished, thus ending the line of the Gjukungs.[151]

Based on these earlier tales, some have theorized that the Burgundians believed that Slagfinn-Gjuki was "their emigration hero and royal progenitor."[152] The preface to the *Lex Burgundionum*, which lists Burgundian kings who have Gjukung names and the *Nibelungenlied*, which makes the Gjukungs, or Gibichungs, the family of the Burgundian kings, seems to support this.[153] Slagfinn-Gjuki was not only a hunter; he was also an archer and a fine musician.[154] His musicianship he passed along to his

---

[151] *The Prose Edda*, 115-117; and *The Saga of the Volsungs: The Saga of Ragnar Lodbrok together with The Lay of Kraka*, trans. Margaret Schlauch, (New York: The AMS Press and W.W. Norton & Company, Inc., 1978; reprint, New York: American-Scandanavian Foundation, vol. 35, Scandinavian Classics, 1930): xvii, (page citations are to the reprint edition), which explained there were other parallels to other Germanic tribes: Jormunrekk, husband of Svanhild, daughter of Sigurd is the historical king of the Goths in southern Russia, Ermanarich, and events surrounding many of these found their way into Jordane's history of the Goths, whose historical accuracy "is open to serious doubt."

[152] Rydberg, *Teutonic Mythology*, 3:1009.

[153] Ibid.

[154] Ibid., 3: 991, 978, 989.

"son," Gunnar, "the greatest player on stringed instruments in the heroic literature. In the den of serpents he still plays his harp, so that the crawling venomous creatures are enchanted by the tones."[155] This defiant act was associated with Gunther, king of the Burgundians, who died at the hands of Etzel in the later compilation, the *Nibelungenlied*.

The Nibelungenlied

Indisputably the Burgundians of Gundahar inspired the later German epic of the Nibelungs. As an anonymous chronicler stated, the historical events of the Burgundian encounter with the Huns must have been memorable to have been used as the basis for the *Nibelungenlied*. Much scholarly work has been done in an attempt to ascertain the degree of historical accuracy in the work.[156] "The *Nibelungenlied* remains, with respect to virtually all aspects of its being hitherto examined by scholars, an enigma, but that is a good, if not the major, part of its attraction for both the academic world as well as that of the educated layman."[157]

---

[155] Ibid., 3:978.

[156] *Chronicle of 452*, in Murray, *Merovingian Gaul*, 83; and Latouche, *Caesar to Charlemagne*, 166-67.

[157] *A Companion to the Nibelungenlied,* ed. Winder McConnell (Columbia, SC: Camden House, 1998), 13; See also a newer work, Francis G. Gentry, Winder McConnell, Ulrich Muller, and Werner Wunderlich, eds., *The Nibelungen Tradition: An Encyclopedia* (New York: Routledge, 2002), which provides a comprehensive resource for guidance in studying the Nibelungenlied. However, also see, Jerold C. Frakes review of the work in *Speculum* 79 (January 2004): 180-2, for the belief that, while the goal was

The *Nibelungenlied* was composed of the two stories previously outlined: one story was about a hero, Sigurd (Sigfrid) and the other story was about a villain, Etzel (Atli), supposedly the historical Attila. The Burgundian kings played the role of antagonist and protagonist, respectively, in each. The story of Sigfrid was often believed to hold little or no historical significance, while the story involving Etzel (Atli) was believed to be at least partially based on the true events surrounding the fall of the Burgundians as it was told in the sixth and seventh centuries. Because of this interpretation of the differing levels of historical accuracy, many believed that the stories were two separate tales combined into one epic. That view has changed in recent years.[158]

To recount the second, and probably more "historic," part of the *Nibelungenlied* briefly, Etzel (Atli/Attila) married Kriemhild (Grimhild/Gudrun), sister of the Burgundian kings and plotted to steal their treasure, symbol of their wealth and power. Etzel (Atli/Attila) invited them to his court while Kriemhild (Grimhild/Gudrun) unsuccessfully attempted to warn her brothers of her husband's plot. A battle ensued upon

---

admirable, the effort generally fell short.

[158] See especially Hugo Bekker, *The Nibelungenlied: a Literary Analysis* (Toronto: University of Toronto Press, 1971), which offered an analysis that demonstrated the parallelism between the two sections and other internal consistencies as exhibited by the descriptions of both courtly and military activities throughout the work; and Frank G. Ryder *The Song of the Nibelungs: A Verse Translation from the Middle High German Nibelungenlied* (Detroit: Wayne State University Press, 1962), 16.

the Burgundian refusal to surrender their treasure and all of them, except Gunther (Gundahar), were killed. Gunther (Gundahar), the last to have knowledge of the whereabouts of the Burgundian treasure, remained defiant in the face of Etzel's (Atli/Attila's) threats, though he was finally killed. Kriemhild (Grimhild/Gudrun) avenged her kin by killing Etzel (Atli/Attila). Finally, in a probable reflection of contemporary rumors that a German bride had killed the historical Attila, Kriemhild (Grimhild/Gudrun) was said to have then burned his hall with his retainers inside. She then threw herself into the flames, ending her own life.[159]

The historical linkages between characters in the poem and those from history have been well documented. Less noticed was an apparent link between the historical Roman general Aëtius and the hero Sigfrid. Both were heroic external forces that brought doom upon the Burgundian state, both were eventually perceived to be threats to the political system, and both of their deaths involved sexual intrigue and vengeful murder.[160]

The obvious historical error of the saga is a case of historical telescoping: the premature placement of Attila as leader of the Huns roughly a generation too soon. However, historical proof of some aspects of the events are extant, i.e. the Burgundians were indeed destroyed by the Huns around A.D. 436, they were led

---

[159] Ryder, *The Song of the Nibelungs*, 34-36.
[160] Brian Murdoch, "Politics in the Niebelungenlied," in *A Companion to the Nibelungenlied*, ed. McConnell, 231-32.

by their king Gundahar, who was killed during these events, and Attila died suddenly in A.D. 453 of a seizure or hemorrhage, possibly brought on by excessive alcoholic consumption. Finally, that the Burgundians had come in contact with, and were influenced by, the Huns has also been shown by their artwork in filigree and by such practices as cranial deformation.[161]

The foundation of the *Nibelungenlied* was built upon the older Germanic myths surrounding Slagfinn-Gjuki. These tales were fused with historical events to produce a heroic tale of epic proportions. However, while certain facts about the Burgundians and Attila may have the ring of truth, the historical value of the *Nibelungenlied* lay more in its reflection of the later chivalric society of the time it was written or compiled.[162]

---

[161] Wolfram, *Germanic Peoples*, 141.

[162] Ryder, *The Song of the Nibelungs*, 16; and Werner Wunderlich, "The Authorship of the Nibelungenlied," in McConnell, ed., *A Companion to the Nibelungenlied*, 251-277, for a summary of the various attempts to determine the author. Wunderlich concluded that the work was written after 1190 and before 1205. Also see J.R.R and Christopher Tolkien, *The Legend of Sigurd and Gudrún* (New York: Harper Collins, 2009), J.R.R. Tolkien believed that the more mythical legends of Sigurd and the Nibelung horde were intertwined with the historical fall of the Burgundians. He based this on a close reading of Anglo-Saxon poetry, particularly *Beowulf* and *Widsith*, as compared to the stories as told in Low or High Germany. From his readings, he concluded that the legend of Sigurd was fit into the fall of the Burgundians because both dealt with some sort of gold hoard. He also offers a theory as to how the Burgundians became known as the Nibelungs. In short, it makes for an interesting, if complicated, read.

Marc A. Comtois

CHAPTER 5
THE FOUNDING AND EARLY DEVELOPMENT OF
THE SECOND BURGUNDIAN KINGDOM
(443 A.D. to 494 A.D.)

Sapaudia

In the Gallic Chronicle of 452, under the year A.D. 443, "Sapaudia was given to the remnants of the Burgundians to be divided with the native inhabitants."[163] Though their first kingdom ended in catastrophic failure, the Burgundians survived. For the twenty years between the fall of the first Burgundian kingdom and the re-settlement in Sapaudia, no Burgundian King has been identified, but in A.D. 456 Gundioc was first mentioned. He may have been related to Gundahar—it seems a stretch of the timeline to place him as a son—or he could have been the scion of a minor line of the Burgundian Gibichungs. It was also possible that he was related to the Goths as stories of the mid-sixth century said that Gundioc was a descendant of the old Goth king Athanaric.[164] The region

---

[163] *Chronicle of 452*, in Murray, *Merovingian Gaul*, 84.

[164] See Wolfram, *Germanic Peoples*, 250, who also stated that "in 457, it was even claimed that the Burgundians were dependent on the Goths of Toulouse." This is doubted by most scholars.

called Sapaudia covered land that now comprises present-day eastern Switzerland and the southern portion of the Jura Mountains, near Geneva. It is generally believed that Aëtius settled the Burgundians in Sapaudia in A.D. 443 because he intended that they serve as a buffer between the Romans of southern Gaul and the traditional Burgundian rivals, the Alamanni, who wanted to expand into the region.[165]

However, others have found it hard to believe that Aëtius would have placed the recently defeated, and thus severely weakened, Burgundians in such an important position along the frontier. Even if the Burgundians were not severely weakened, it is doubtful that a brilliant tactician such as Aëtius would have placed a strong and resentful Burgundian tribe in a strategic position. Thus, instead of the Alamanni, the problem was probably the rebellious Bacaudae and their allies in Gaul. Aëtius had settled the Visigoths in Aquitannia to quell a similar uprising at about the same time. Given this, the Burgundians, though still weakened by their encounter with Aëtius and the Huns, were of sufficient strength to deal effectively with a peasant and slave uprising. Finally, they were in no position to

---

[165] Musset, *Germanic Invasions*, 63; and Edward James, *The Origins of France: From Clovis to the Capetians, 500-1000* (New York: St. Martin's Press, 1982), 22, are examples of the generally accepted reason for the settlement of the Burgundians in Sapaudia; and Anthony King, *Roman Gaul and Germany* (Berkeley: University of California Press, 1990), 209. King believed these buffer zones could have contributed to the development of a cultural frontier in later France, as it serves as a rough demarcation between where the langue d'oil and the langue doc was spoken.

pressure Rome into settling them on new lands.[166]

The relationship of the Bishop Hilary of Arles and Aëtius has also been proposed as a reason for the relocation of the Burgundians to Sapaudia. Hilary enjoyed widespread ecclesiastical support in the region, with a strong base centered at Lerins. He also had strong secular support outside of his own province. One of his strongest proponents was Aëtius, who could have moved the Burgundians to Sapaudia to protect Hilary while he was at Besançon.[167] This latter theory does not necessarily exclude the possibility that the Burgundians were placed in the region to quell a rebellion. Taken together, both may offer a more plausible scenario than that of a weakened people being placed in a key

---

[166] E.A. Thompson, "The Settlement of the Barbarians in Southern Gaul," *The Journal of Roman Studies* 46, parts 1 and 2 (1956): 67, 69, 71-72, 74; Justine Davis Randers-Pehrson, *Barbarians and Romans: The Birth Struggle of Europe, A.D. 400-700*, (Norman: University of Oklahoma Press, 1983): 190, concurred with Thompson's theory of protection against local brigands, though she believed they also were needed to guard against incursions from other barbarian groups; and J.M. Wallace-Hadrill, *The Long-Haired Kings and other studies in Frankish History*, (New York: Barnes & Noble, Inc., 1962): 28, offered the thoroughly contrarian, and perhaps most measured, statement that no one knew precisely why the Burgundians were settled in "Savoy" by Aëtius in A.D. 443. Despite some peasant unrest, Savoy didn't seem to be in any danger of internal uprising and the Alamans were possibly too far away to pose an immediate threat.

[167] See Mathisen, *Ecclesiastical Factionalism*, 153-57, especially n. 62, which referred to Heinzelmann, *Bischofsherrschaft in Gallien: Zur Kontinuitat romischer Fuhrungsschichten von 4. Bis zum 7. Jahrhundert* (Munich, 1976), 83; and Georg Langgartner, *Die Galliepolitik der Papste im 5. Und 6. Jahrhundert. Eine Studie uber den apostolische Vikariat von Arles* (Bonn, 1964), 74-77, the latter believed that Aëtius' motivation for moving the Burgundians to Sapaudia was related to his relationship to Hilary.

defensive position within the empire.

There are other theories. Some believe the Burgundians were too unsophisticated to realize they were being played as dupes by Aëtius. As proof, the earlier Burgundian support for Jovinus has been cited. According to this theory, the Burgundians were too naïve in imperial politics to realize that they were being rebellious against Rome. Accordingly, the Burgundians applied a kind of circular logic whereby Jovinus was a legitimate emperor because he said he was and, thus, their support for him was legitimate. This was despite the fact that he had claimed the throne in large part because of Burgundian support. Thus, with the precedent of a Burgundian collective of circular logicians established, some historians have suggested that Aëtius cleverly placed these "loyal if naïve barbarians" in an area that needed to be protected while simultaneously implying to the Gallic aristocrats that these same barbarians may be manipulated or agree with them on a grander plan for Gauls' place within the empire.[168]

Another, perhaps more likely reason, was that Aëtius realized the benefit of having the allegiance and obligations, guaranteed under *foederati* status, of a group of barbarians who knew what it meant to face the Huns. Perhaps Aëtius was even clever enough to realize that the Huns were getting too powerful and were a potential problem with whom he would soon have to deal. The Burgundians were only one of a few key alliances he made to vouchsafe against an eventual loss

---

[168] Randers-Pehrson, *Barbarians and Romans*, 192.

of the control of his Hunnish mercenaries. On the Burgundian's part, the desire to ingratiate themselves with Rome also cannot be discounted, thus they may have not been so much naïve as having few other options.[169]

Whether the Burgundians were settled to perform their duties as garrison troops, constables, or bodyguards, they were eventually called upon by Aëtius to provide warriors for military action in other regions of Gaul. In A.D. 451, a faction of Burgundians followed Aëtius and Theodoric, king of the Visigoths, when they faced Attila and his Huns and allies on the Catalaunian Plains, near the city of Troyes (or Chalons). Another faction of Burgundians joined Attila. Attila's Burgundians were from among those that still lived on the eastern shore of the Rhine and were part of the Hun army that entered the Belgic provinces, took Metz on April 7, 451, and pillaged and burned many other cities.[170]

Attila's Burgundians probably split from the main body during the Vandal assault of A.D. 406. These were the Burgundians who had purportedly turned to Christianity after defeating the Hun Uptar, but later must have been defeated and integrated into the Hunnic horde.[171] Their existence lends credence to the theory

---

[169] Ibid.

[170] See Jordanes, *Goths*, 30; Bury, *Invasion of Europe,* 146-49; and Wolfram, *Germanic Peoples*, 136, for the presence of Burgundians among Attila's forces.

[171] Thompson, *A History of Attila and the Huns*, 136; and Wolfram, *Germanic Peoples*, 251, who believed that this group seems to have slowly

that Germanic tribes didn't operate in the classically believed mono-ethnic manner. Germans prioritized booty and strength over racial or social loyalty.

Aëtius's tactic of pitting one Germanic tribe against another, while often successful, resulted in serious repercussions for the Roman Empire. The Empire's policy of employing barbarians as mercenaries resulted in the gradual consolidation of military power into the hands of various barbarian generals. Roman rulers had concluded that it was safer to have foreign defenders in lieu of Roman armies because foreign chiefs were excluded by their nationality from having a legitimate claim on the throne.[172]

They attracted these chiefs by settling their people on Roman lands and extracting a pledge that they and their people would protect Rome from foreign invaders. The specific nature of the Roman practice of providing land, or some other form of payment, to barbarians in return for their service as defenders has been much debated by historians. All agree that the Roman legal concept called *hospitalitas* played a role in this mixing of Germans and Romans within a province, but there has been disagreement over the specific characteristics of this system.

The system of *hospitalitas* was used to settle the

---

dispersed after the defeat of Attila, and some of them eventually found their way to the kingdom of their tribesmen along the Rhone.

[172] C. Delisle Burns, "Christianity and the First Europe," in *The Barbarian Invasions: Catalyst of a New Order*, ed. Katherine Fischer Drew (New York: Holt, Rinehart and Winston, 1970), 109-10.

Burgundians in their new kingdom of Sapaudia in A.D. 443. Earlier historians believed that Rome gave one-third to two-thirds of the Roman landowners' estates, including the people on them, to the Germanic troops billeted there. More recent studies have theorized that, while there was probably a system of land allotment, this evolved into a system of tax revenue transfer. The Burgundians, and other Germanic tribes, were actually given a fixed portion of taxes assessed on land held by Romans rather than a portion of the actual land thus occupied. Finally, this transfer of tax revenue was made easier because the collection and distribution stayed in the hands of the Roman municipal office holders, the *curiales*, and did not fall to the barbarians themselves.[173]

Over the years, the Burgundian king gave royal gifts and every loyal Burgundian retainer gained land to go with their share of the tax revenue, if they had not received land already. This informal system turned the Burgundians into landowners. Further, in a series of trade-offs with Roman landowners, they consolidated and centralized their estates, as did the Romans, and "a

---

[173] Musset, *Germanic Invasions*, 64; Collins, *Early Medieval Europe*, 227; and see especially Goffart, *Barbarians and Romans*, 160-1. Initially, the barbarians were assigned to a specific locality, given shelter and provisioned. The rations shortly changed to allotments, based on landed security and involving some sort of relationship to one or more Roman landowners, though it was primarily revenue, not really property in the sense of land, that changed hands. This enabled the Roman government to remove itself as a middleman from the equation and charged the Roman landowners to pay a percentage directly to the barbarians; see Wolfram, *Germanic Peoples*, 112-113, who also agrees with Goffart's interpretation; and Geary, *The Myth of Nations*, 103.

new, Romano-Burgundian amalgam of landlords came into existence."[174]

These results caused confusion in later historical analysis as they were taken to be the form of the original design rather than the evolved result. Additionally, the system of tax reapportionment made sense because settled Barbarian troops did not cost anymore to the taxpayers than Roman troops. Finally, the "dignity and eminence" of the existing aristocracies and clergy were not adversely affected by the presence of these barbarians.[175]

The acute instinct of the vastly outnumbered Burgundians to be inoffensive to the Gallo-Romans probably helped them gain the acceptance of their more tenured neighbors.[176] Some believed that the Gallo-Romans even welcomed any Germans as a new source of manpower to till Roman lands, or that, specifically in the Burgundians case, that old memories of joining together in support of Jovinus had eased the way for sharing Roman lands.[177] That there were barbarians within the Roman Empire prior to the "invasions,"

---

[174] Goffart, "Rome, Constantinople, and the Barbarians," 295.

[175] Goffart, "Rome, Constantinople, and the Barbarians," 295; and Gordon, "Subsidies in Roman Imperial Defence," 69, who noted of the barbarians that "when they finally occupied the Roman lands of the west, they had reached a state of civilization which enabled them to appreciate and to make some effort to preserve the civilization they had taken over. This is to be credited in large measure to the subsidies they had received for so long."; see a more detailed discussion on Gallo-Romans and Burgundians below, 99.

[176] James, *The Origins of France*, 22.

[177] Randers-Pehrson, *Barbarians and Romans*, 190.

mostly former or current members of the Roman army or prisoners and their descendents who had been used to repopulate militarily devastated regions, has also been shown.[178] Finally, it has been determined that the Burgundians modified their military unit structure to include Gallo-Romans within the ranks. As such, military, and later political, command, originally in the hands of chiefs or strong warriors who led *comitatus*, fell to the counts, or *comes*, of both Romans and Burgundians.[179]

While the Burgundians attempted to smooth relations between their tribe and their Gallo-Roman neighbors, they also took proactive steps to maintain their own tribal unity within their new kingdom. They prescribed common laws and fostered a "common sense of identity" among their Germanic population while at the same time they tried to segregate between the Germans and the Roman or Gallo-Roman people who made up the majority of their new lands. Part of this Germanic unification process was accomplished by kings associating themselves with heroes of often mythical royal families or, at the very least, storied families from the history of their people,[180] as did the Burgundian kings by associating themselves with the Gibichungs.

Most of the German tribes used religion as a

---

[178] Musset, *Germanic Invasions*, 162-64.

[179] Ibid., 173.

[180] See Geary, *The Myth of Nations*, 108, who noted that, for the most part, Arianism was a relatively benign faith as practiced by the Germans, and any Catholics within the kingdoms were usually tolerated, even when they were other Germans.

unifying element. Since most tribes, including the Burgundians, were Arian, this heretical Christianity became a cultural unifier. It was especially identified with the members of the royal families.[181] The Burgundians also established law codes that drew from both traditional Germanic codes and probably some "local vulgar" Roman law traditions.[182] Finally, while these actions and beliefs were true for the free men who fought for their king, the opinions and thoughts of the peasants and slaves will probably never be known.[183]

Expansion into Gaul

The traditional political groups interested in the western imperial regimes of the first half of the fifth century were the Eastern Empire, the Roman armies and the Roman and Gallic senators. After about A.D. 450, the barbarian groups that had been established on Roman territory (including the Burgundians) had to be added to this mix. After the death of Attila in A.D. 453 and his greatest sponsor Aëtius in A.D. 454, the Huns were no longer a factor in Roman politics. The only sensible course of action was to include some of the barbarian groups in the political machinations of the time.[184]

Some accounts state that a Burgundian king, Gundicar (often confused or conflated with Gundahar)

---

[181] Geary, *The Myth of Nations*, 108-9.
[182] Ibid., 109.
[183] Ibid., 174.
[184] Heather, "The Huns," 31.

had fallen to Attila's horde at Troyes/Chalons and his sons Gundioc and Chilperic I assumed leadership of the Burgundians. They supported Avitus, a Gallic aristocrat who had been appointed master of soldiers in A.D. 455, as candidate for emperor when news came to Toulouse that the Emperor Maximus had been killed by the Vandal sack of Rome in A.D. 455. Avitus' candidacy was also supported by the Franks and he was declared Roman Emperor by the Gallo-Roman senators on July 9, 455.[185] Also in this year, the Gepids were driven back by the Burgundians and dispersed through Gaul.[186]

The raising of Avitus to the purple was the conclusion of a process that had been developing in Gaul for some time. The provinces in Gaul had been administered semi-autonomously from the imperial government prior to the late fourth and fifth centuries, but any pebble thrown into the center of the Imperial pool made waves that eventually reached the outer edges. All of the trials and tribulations that were endured by Rome were also felt by her provinces. The Gallic aristocracy saw the imperial court abandon Trier, heard the barbarians pounding on their gates, and felt

---

[185] Ibid., 32-3.

[186] *Avitus of Vienne*, 15. Shanzer and Wood convincingly argued that while the *Continuatio Havniensis Prosperi* stated that the Burgundians were dispersed throughout Gaul because they "were driven back by the Gepids,…It would make more sense if the Gepids rather than the Burgundians were the subject of the verb *repelluntur*." Thus, the Gepids were driven by the Burgundians, and not the other way around. The apparent misstatement in the *Continuatio Havniensis Prosper* is a clear example of the confusions and ambiguities associated with the sources which contribute to the Burgundians being lost in the mist of time.

the tension between the Eastern and Western imperial courts after the death of Theodosious. An attitude of self-reliance was born, though interest in the machinations of imperial politics was still keen as Gallo-Romans continued to participate in imperial factional politics.[187] The raising of the Gallo-Roman Avitus as emperor was the pinnacle of their efforts.

Gundioc and Chilperic I then accompanied the Visigothic king Theodoric II (A.D. 453-466) on his campaign against the Suevi in Spain (A.D. 456), which he undertook at the behest of Avitus. Together, the Burgundians and Visigoths fought the entire tribe of the Suevi near the river Ulbius and almost destroyed them. Unfortunately for Avitus, the Eastern Empire did not support him and Majorian and Ricimer, Roman-barbarian generals, deposed him at Placentia, where he was made a bishop and died soon after.[188]

Ricimer

There were two legitimate Roman generals considered to be both militarily and politically strong enough to attract a following in Gaul and to be viable candidates for emperor. The first was Marcellinus, who was supported by both Gallo-Roman aristocrats and the

---

[187] P.S. Barnwell, *Emperor, Prefects, & Kings: The Roman West, 395-565* (Chapel Hill: The University of North Carolina Press, 1992), 68.

[188] Jordanes, *Goths*, 36; and *Chronica a. CCCCLV-DLXXXI*, ed. Th. Mommsen, *Chronica Minora 2, MGH AA 11* (1894), 225-39; and *La Chronique de Marius d'Avenches (455-581)*, ed. and trans. Justin Favrod, 2nd ed. (Lausannne, 1993) trans. A.C. Murray in Murray, *Merovingian Gaul*, 101. Hereafter cited as *Marius of Avenches*.

Burgundians in Lyons. The other was the Roman general Marjorian who had the support of his barbarian colleague Ricimer. To prevent conflict, Marcellinus decided to support Marjorian, a friend as well as a rival, in his bid for Emperor. His Gallo-Roman followers were not so understanding and continued to agitate for Marcellinus after Marjorian's ascendence to the throne. For this continuing intransigence, Marjorian burdened them with heavy taxes.[189]

In A.D. 457, the Burgundians seized large portions of Lugdunensis I and Viennensis, apparently as a form of self-payment for their just concluded service to the Empire. They were aided by an uprising in Lugdunum (Lyons) and proceeded to occupy the city, probably at the invitation of the Gallo-Romans.[190] Marjorian gathered an army to move against them, but they withdrew, either because of fear of Marjorian's army or because of diplomacy undertaken on Marjorian's behalf. Majorian, not confident in the strength of his army, lobbied the Burgundians and gained their support. However, despite any agreement, the Burgundians soon returned to Lyons and took the city, perhaps as early as A.D. 461, but no later than A.D. 474. They continued to expand in this period, taking Die in A.D. 463, Vaison before A.D. 474 and Langres before A.D. 485. [191]

---

[189] Randers-Pehrson, *Barbarians and Romans*, 252.

[190] "In this year [A.D. 456] the Burgundians took part of Gaul and divided the lands with the Gallic senators." *Marius of Avenches* in Murray, *Merovingian Gaul*, 101.

[191] Sidonius alluded to both the efforts of an Imperial Secretary,

Some of these land grabbing movements could be attributed to the political machinations of Ricimer. Marjorian was but one of many subsequent puppet emperors put up by Ricimer. Ricimer disposed of Marjorian and Marcellinius refused to recognize the next puppet, Severus. Instead, Marcellinius went to Dalmatia where he posed an immediate threat to the Ravenna-seated government of Ricimer. Ricimer's position was made more precarious because Marcellinius also had the protection of the Eastern emperor and he was also under threat from the west by Marjorian's former general Aegidius. For help, Ricimer enlisted the aid of the Burgundians.[192]

Ricimer was a master propagandist and successfully portrayed Aegidius as an upstart and replaced him with the Burgundian king Gundioc, no later than A.D. 463, who he moved into the strategically well-placed Lyons. He also convinced the Visigoths that his choice for emperor, Severus, was the rightful one. This forced Aegidius to seek allies, including the Franks from

---

Petrus, to secure Burgundian support for Marjorian and that Burgundians marched under Marjorian's standard in later action in his *Poems and Letters*. trans. and intro. by W.B. Anderson, vol.1, Loeb Classical Library (Cambridge, Mass.: Harvard University Press, 1936), 1:102-11; and Ian Wood, *The Merovingian Kingdoms, 450-751* (London: Longman Group, 1995), 9-10, in which it was observed that, "For the most part...the Burgundians were among the most loyal federates of the Empire, and they were proud of their connections with the Romans. The conflict with Majorian was caused by his reversal of the policies of Avitus, rather than any hostility towards the Empire held by the Burgundians themselves."; also see Musset, *Germanic Invasions*, 63; and Wolfram, *Germanic Peoples*, 251-52, for further exposition.

[192] Randers-Pehrson, *Barbarians and Romans*, 252.

Tournai, under the Merovingian chief Childeric. Ricimer and his allies eventually prevailed, but these events set the stage for further antagonism between the Franks, Visigoths and Burgundians.[193] Further, as a reward for his help, Ricimer formally awarded Gundioc with Aegidius's former position of master of soldiers (*magister militum*), while he ceded control of Narbonne to Theoderic II.[194]

In fact, every subsequent Roman regime lobbied support from Gallo-Roman and Italian senators, Goths, Franks and Burgundians. This resulted in a policy among the Germans of withholding support for an imperial figurehead unless a proper payoff was promised. The Burgundian kings won Roman titles as Gundioc, Chilperic I and later Gundobad, were all regarded as patricians of Gaul. By the time of the Emperor Anthemius (A.D. 467-472), large concessions had been made to the Burgundians in Gaul to ensure their aid against Euric and his Goths.[195]

These events reveal that the Burgundians were active participants in imperial faction politics. They apparently felt that standing in the Empire and relations with respect to the Emperor were important. Their earlier military actions confirm this. They supported the

---

[193] Ibid., 255.

[194] A.H.M. Jones, *The Later Roman Empire, 284-602: a Social, Economic and Administrative Survey*, 3 vols, (Oxford, 1964): 241-2, in Barnwell, *Emperor, Prefects, & Kings*, 82.

[195] Heather, "The Huns," 32-33; Mathisen, *Roman Aristocrats*, 83; Bury, *Roman Empire*, 1:339; and Randers-Pehrson, *Barbarians and Romans*, 255.

Romans against the Suevi in the 450s and the Huns in A.D. 452 and sided with one emperor against the followers of a deposed other when they fought Aegidius. They may have seized Lyons after Avitus was deposed because the Gallic senators supported the late emperor and opposed Marjorian. They also must have been viewed as powerful political players in the empire if the Gallo-Roman aristocrat Arvandus approached them to propose that they be given territory in exchange for supporting the removal of Anthemius.[196]

Gallo-Romans and Burgundians

Concessions to barbarians in the form of lands and titles were a necessity for the Empire. However, the constant rebellions for expansion strained the imperial treasury and the Empire taxed the goods produced by its territories to pay for the army and its administration. At the same time, the Empire was giving away either land or the tax revenue it generated, which reduced the resources available for defense and civil service. This reduction in resources significantly affected the Roman elite.

By the fourth century, as the church had expanded and the Roman bureaucracy shrank, Roman aristocrats became attracted to ecclesiastical offices as a means of exercising local political power. As a result, the

---

[196] Barnwell, *Emperor, Prefects, & Kings*, 83; and Sidonius, *The Letters of Sidonius*, trans. O.M. Dalton, 2 vols. (Oxford, 1915) in Murray, *Merovingian Gaul*, 207-10. That the Burgundians were enmeshed in imperial politics to a great degree is also supported by the observations found in Wood, *The Merovingian Kingdoms,* 15.

line between imperial politics and ecclesiastical administration became blurred. There were also many who sought these offices for more traditional, spiritual reasons and some, such as Martin of Tours and Ambrose of Milan, opposed imperial interference in Church affairs, though others, such as Felix of Trier, supported secular involvement in administration. The Roman aristocratic class relied on imperial careers for prestige and class legitimization as well as moneymaking opportunities.[197] The weakening of the Roman Empire, perceived by the lessening of revenue by these elites, weakened the attachment between them and Rome. Eventually, loyalty to Rome served no practical purpose and the elite landowners began to look to the barbarians who lived among them to preserve their societal standing and property.[198]

This atmosphere prompted Salvian of Marseille, writing in the 440s, to observe that many Romans fled to the barbarian lands, despite their different religious beliefs. These Romans "prefer to live as free people under an outward form of captivity than as captives under an appearance of liberty."[199] As such, the idea of being a Roman citizen, once coveted, was abandoned. Gallo-Roman aristocrats perceived a lack of imperial interest in maintaining Gaul at the level they expected and this may have tended to both unify the Gallo-

---

[197] Mathisen, "The Gallic Church In The Fourth Century," in *Ecclesiastical Factionalism*, 5-26.

[198] Heather, "The Huns," 21-22.

[199] *The Writings of Salvian the Presbyter*, trans. Jeremiah F. O'Sullivan, (New York, 1947) in Murray, *Merovingian Gaul*, 120.

Romans and separate them from others of their class who lived in other parts of the empire.[200]

By the time the Burgundians entered Gaul, the Gallo-Romans had already begun to think of themselves less as Romans, more as Gauls and more interested in their own immediate concerns than in preserving the concept of empire. Additionally, though they loved Rome, self-interested Gallo-Romans had considered a strong central government not in their best interests and a threat to their family-based commercial and political oligarchy. Aristocrats who assessed their situation and reacted appropriately often survived the barbarian conquerors and even profited from them.[201] However, this did not mean that they lost faith in the Roman method of government. "Where Romans were in charge, it is not unreasonable to suppose that 'Roman' governmental traditions were continued at the local level."[202]

While this Gallo-Roman flexibility contributed to their survival, it could not have succeeded without an accommodating barbarian king and his people. From their first contact with Rome, barbarians had been cognizant of the advantage of life in the Empire. Regardless of the exact nature of their entrance into the Empire, whether as raiders or *foederati* or refugees, they sought land of their own. "They were likely to look for

---

[200] Mathisen, *Roman Aristocrats*, 18-20.
[201] Geary, *Before France and Germany,* 92-3; and Mathisen, *Roman Aristocrats*, 71.
[202] Barnwell, *Emperors, Prefects, & Kings*, 70.

militarily and economically secure places to settle, and to seek integration with the native population."[203]

The Burgundians were a small tribe and realized that they could not simply overwhelm the traditional inhabitants of any region in which they were settled. In addition, at least one of their traditions claimed they were genealogically related to the Romans.[204] As such, in the case of the Burgundian kingdom, there was no social differentiation made between Gallo-Roman or Burgundian. Roman senators and Burgundian nobles were considered of a class, and this equality between social strata held true down to the lowest classes of both people. Additionally, the Burgundian kingdom was administered similarly to a traditional Roman province. It was composed of *civitates*, which were the same as the episcopal dioceses, and was administered by both a Burgundian and a Roman official.[205]

The new Roman aristocratic clergymen sought barbarian patronage. For instance, Pope Hilarus wrote to Leontius of Arles about a complaint concerning Mamertus of Vienne's ordination of a new bishop, Marcellus, for the city of Die. In a letter dated October 10, 463, Hilarus explained that he heard of this from his "son, the illustrious master of soldiers Gundioc"[206] who

---

[203] Ibid., 171.

[204] Wolfram, *Germanic Peoples*, 259.

[205] Ibid., 258.

[206] *Hil.Epist.* "Qualiter contra sedis" (MGH Epist. 3.28-29) in Mathisen, *Roman Aristocrats*, 73. Mathisen noted how Thiel, *Epistolae*, 147, note 3 "interprets the appellation filius noster used by Hilarus of Gundioc to mean that Gundioc was Catholic at the time."

also said that Marcellus was named bishop against the wishes of the inhabitants of Die.

This amply illustrated that Gundioc was not only the new Burgundian king of Die, but was also a Roman official and sent a report to Hilarus that prompted the Pope's action. Whether Gundioc directed his report to the Pope because he was the leader of the ecclesiastics and logical choice to address the matter or because Gundioc was a Catholic and naturally deferred to the Pope remains unknown. Gundioc's position as both king and Roman official probably complicated the networks of loyalty, patronage, and authority at Die. Nonetheless, this Burgundian king filled the void left by the removal of Gallo-Roman patrons and often heard Gallo-Roman appeals.[207]

That Gundioc held the position of both Burgundian king and the Roman office of *magister militum per Gallias* reveals the degree of assimilation achieved by the Burgundians, something that neither the Visigoths nor Franks had yet accomplished.[208] Thus, the Burgundian kings held a definite place in the imperial hierarchy and this led to the Gallo-Romans accepting the legitimacy of the Burgundian royal court as the locus of provincial government. This peaceful coexistence resulted in very little direct conflict between Burgundians and the Roman Empire: Burgundians only

---

[207] Mathisen, *Roman Aristocrats*, 73-74.

[208] H. Elton, "Defence in fifth century Gaul," 172, in *Fifth-century Gaul: a Crisis of Identity?*, eds. Drinkwater and Elton; and Barnwell, *Emperors, Prefects, & Kings*, 82.

fought Romans once, at Lyons in A.D. 458 against Marjorian.[209]

Another account told of the charity of the Gallo-Roman senator Ecdicius during a famine in Burgundy. Ecdicius sent his men with wagons to gather the starving people to his estate and fed and lodged four thousand until the famine was over. He then returned them home. There were other reports of how Ecdicius was a leader and man of action, as indicated by a story of how he repelled a party of Goths with only ten other men. Another Gallo-Roman, Patiens, Bishop of Lyons, helped people avert starvation in a like manner. These stories show the charity of the Gallo-Romans as well as their ability to maintain their comfortable lifestyle under the "harsh rule" of barbarian kings.[210]

Church officials could also successfully petition barbarian kings for relief. In the 460s, the abbot Lupicinus of St. Claude asked the Burgundian king

---

[209] Elton, "Defence in Fifth Century Gaul," 175, also believed that this lack of military confrontation also masked the military weakness of the less-populous Burgundians.

[210] Gregory of Tours, *The History of the Franks*, 137-8; and see Samual Dill, "Persistence of the Aristocratic Way of Life," in *The Barbarian Invasions: Catalyst of a New Order*, ed. Katherine Fischer Drew (New York: Holt, Rinehart and Winston, 1970), 17. Dill observed that the higher clergy, such as Ecdicius and Patiens, came mostly from wealthy, aristocratic families and they played prominent parts in the politics of the time. They used their power and wealth to preserve the Roman tradition, which maintained their position in society; Bury, *Roman Empire*, 1:342; and Whittaker, *Frontiers of the Roman Empire*, 273, for the point that only those soldiers who "rate[d] a mention" were mentioned in the account of Ecdicius and his defense against the Goths. In essence, only the "knights," not their "retainers" and "squires," were mentioned.

Chilperic I to free some paupers who claimed that they had been illegally enslaved. The oppressor of these peasants was a Roman "sycophant" according to the Gallo-Roman writer Sidonius. As a means of defense, the accused Roman official attempted to smear the abbot by charging that Lupicinus had predicted the ruin of the Burgundians ten years prior. Lupicinus accused the King and his tribe of oppressing the poor against the wishes of Rome. The king was affected by the plea of the abbot and offered land and vineyards to the monastery as recompense.[211] This act of impartial justice toward a Catholic abbot by a supposed Arian king stood the Burgundian royalty in good stead among Catholics, especially as compared to other barbarian Arians, such as the Goths.

Records show that Gallo-Roman families continued to be influential, and wealthy, for generations. Some transferred their service from the state to the church, though many became gradually accepted into Burgundian service, serving as counts (*comes*), treasurers or in other positions, with some offices designated only for those who were Roman by birth. Their influence upon the administration of the Burgundian kingdom was evident, for instance, the Burgundians continued to use consular years to date administrative documents, still written in Latin.[212]

---

[211] *Vulpicini* 10 in Mathisen, *Roman Aristocrats*, 101; and Dill, *Roman Society*, 37.

[212] Dill, *Roman Society*, 38; See Mathisen, *Roman Aristocrats*, 128-29, for specific examples of Roman aristocrats who filled positions in Burgundian government; for a particular focus on the use of Latin during

One major difference between Burgundian and Roman rule was the development of the office of *comes* into a dual position of both military officer and civil servant. This was antithetical to the standard of separation of powers that had been the imperial policy since Diocletian. These representatives of Roman culture greatly influenced the Burgundians and also benefited from the relationship, as did the Catholic church, which experienced an upsurge in church building under the Arian Burgundians. [213]

Sidonius wrote often about his Burgundian overlords and was both complimentary and derogatory in his remarks. He described the wedding of a Burgundian Princess in which the groom was "in flame-red mantle, with much glint of ruddy gold, and gleam of snowy silken tunic, his fair hair, red cheeks and white skin according with the three hues of his equipment." [214]

---

this period see Yitzhak Hen, *Culture and Religion in Merovingian Gaul A.D. 481-751* (Leiden: E.J. Brill, 1995), 24-7. Hen has suggested that there is little doubt that Latin was the language spoken in Burgundy throughout the Merovingian period, giving as evidence the literary works produced during the era.

[213] For the end of separation of powers in the position of the *comes* see Louis Halphen, "Germanic Society in the Early Sixth Century," in *The Barbarian Invasions: Catalyst of a New Order*, ed. Katherine Fischer Drew (New York: Holt, Rinehart and Winston, 1970), 29; also see the Preface of the Burgundian Code (1.14) in which are listed the names of thirty one counts who appended their seals to the Constitution in *The Burgundian Code*, trans. Katherine Fischer Drew with a foreword by Edward Peters, 4th ed. (Philadelphia: University of Pennsylvania Press, 1992), 21; For the apparent upsurge in church building, see King, *Roman Gaul*, 193-94. King surveyed archeological evidence in Lyons that indicated an upsurge in church building in the mid-fifth century.

[214] Sidonius, *The Letters of Sidonius*, 215-16.

The guards who walked with him were more martial in appearance:

> Their feet were laced in boots of bristly hide reaching to the heels; ankles and legs were exposed. They wore high tight tunics of varied colour, hardly descending to the bare knees, the sleeves covering only the upper arm. Green mantles they had with crimson borders; baldrics supported swords hung from their shoulders, and pressed on sides covered with cloaks of skin secured by brooches. No small part of their adornment consisted of their arms; in their hands they grasped barbed spears and missile axes; their left sides were guarded by shields which flashed with tawny golden bosses and snowy silver borders, betraying at once their wealth and their good taste.[215]

However, not all Burgundians had similar fashion sense, as Sidonius also wrote of how his seven-foot Burgundian patrons of Lyons reeked of garlic and onions

---

[215] Sidonius, *The Letters of Sidonius*, 215-16; and Edward James, *The Franks* (Oxford, UK: Basil Blackwell Ltd., 1988), 74, believed this wedding is evidence of a possible marriage alliance between the Burgundians and the Salian Franks engineered by Ricimer and the Burgundians to unite against the Alamans around 469. James believed that Sidonius' account of the wedding of the Frankish prince Sigismer was "an interesting corrective to the view that late Romans viewed barbarians with distaste."

and spread butter in their hair. Additionally, he seemed to write from personal experience when he complained of having to feed them breakfast, which required a generous amount of food.[216]

He also related to Auspicius, bishop of Toul that he had written a letter to Felix of Narbonne that said, "I have less opportunity to enjoy the blessed contemplation of your presence, fearing at one time harm from my neighbors [the Visigoths], and at another resentment from my patrons [the Burgundians]."[217] Despite Sidonius's derogatory remarks, he also praised the Burgundians and preferred their rule to that of the Visigothic King Euric, which he endured for a time. Confirmation of this belief can be seen by Sidonius' account of the actions of two of his relatives who moved into Burgundian lands in the 460s because they preferred Burgundian to Visigothic rule.[218]

Most Gallo-Romans hoped that Burgundian power would counter the expansionist desires of the Visigothic king Euric. The aristocratic families in Roman Gaul adjusted to Burgundian rule by restructuring the methods and institutions to better suit the new situation. While the senatorial families of Gaul had withstood the barbarian occupation and some had even thrived, the political positions and patronage that had been in place under the Empire vanished.[219] As a result,

---

[216] Ibid., 213.

[217] Sidonius, *Epist. 7.II.I* in Mathisen, *Roman Aristocrats*, 29.

[218] Sidonius, *Epist. 7.II.I* in Mathisen, *Roman Aristocrats*, 29; and Mathisen, *Roman Aristocrats*, 64.

[219] *Avitus of Vienne*, 6.

they regarded the ecclesiastical offices as a suitable, if not the only, replacement for an aristocratic hierarchy.[220] However, these aristocrats were also hindered by the new barriers placed between them by the new barbarian states, which made it more difficult to cultivate and maintain a network of political and personal relationships without risking the suspicion of the various barbarian kings who now ruled the land.[221]

---

[220] See Mathisen, *Roman Aristocrats*, 144, who stated that Gallo-Romans moved into ecclesiastical offices in pursuit of a "general aristocratic ideology. Virtually all of the material and psychological needs of secular aristocracy were available in the church." This may be true, but reducing their motivations as strictly materialistic discounts the very real possibility that they actually wanted to serve both their communities and the church. *Noblesse oblige* was an important component of the Gallo-Roman aristocratic ideology.

[221] *Avitus of Vienne*, 6.

CHAPTER 6
GUNDOBAD'S RISE TO POWER
(472 A.D. TO 494 A.D.)

Roman Patrician

During this time, the Burgundians were threatened by the Visigothic king Euric, who had succeeded his brother Theodoric II as king of the Visigoths in A.D. 472 under suspicious circumstances. Euric made forays into Gaul and seized Bourges and Arles and rampaged along the Rhône valley. Fear of immediate, prolonged war with the Burgundians tempered his actions, but he left the land in tatters and facing imminent famine.[222] Around A.D. 470, Gundioc died and was succeeded by his brother Chilperic I, who, , if actions are any indicator, took his duty as an imperial federate seriously. Chilperic pushed the attacking Visigoths out of the lower Rhône Valley, but devastated the surrounding countryside in the process, which hit the Gallo-Romans especially hard.[223]

Meanwhile, Gundobad, second son of Gundioc,

---

[222] It was during this time that the archbishop Patiens gathered and dispersed food throughout the countryside at his own expense.

[223] Jordanes, *Goths*, 36; Bury, *Roman Empire*, 1:342-43; and Wolfram, *Germanic Peoples*, 252.

had joined the imperial service as a protégé of his uncle, Ricimer the Patrician of Rome. In A.D. 472, the Italian peninsula was essentially divided into two kingdoms. One ruled by the Western Emperor, Anthemius, in Rome while the other was ruled by Ricimer in Milan. Ricimer, who was Anthemius's son-in-law, raised Olybrius as Western Emperor, attacked Anthemius' forces in Rome and was victorious. Anthemius disguised himself and hid in the church of St. Chrysogonus after his supporters surrendered to Ricimer. His disguise failed and he was discovered and killed by Ricimer and Gundobad.[224]

Ricimer died six weeks after the death of Anthemius and Emperor Olybrius replaced him with Gundobad. Upon Olybrius's own death in A.D. 473, Gundobad selected an unknown named Glycerius as his candidate for Emperor of the West. Glycerius, perhaps in a show of gratitude, also appointed one of the Gundobad's kinsmen, either Chilperic I (Gundobad's uncle) or Chilperic II (Gundobad's brother), as master of soldiers in Gaul, based in Lyons, in A.D. 474.[225] The

[224] See Bury, *Invasion of Europe* (164) for the explanation that Ricimer's sister was wife to Gundioc, Gundobad's father. Thus, Ricimer was Gundobad's uncle; and *Chronica Gallica, DXI*, ed. Th. Mommsen *Chronica Minora I, MGH AA 9* (1892), 664-666, trans. A.C. Murray in Murray, *Merovingian Gaul*, 99. (Hereafter cited as *Chronicle of 511*); *Avitus of Vienne*, 15-16; and Barnwell, *Emperor, Prefects, & Kings*, 83.

[225] See Barnwell, *Emperor, Prefects, & Kings*, 83, who, following many before him, believed that this title was conferred upon Chilperic I, Gundobad's uncle and brother to Gundioc, as a reward for defending against the Visigoths in the Rhone valley around A.D. 470. However, also see *Avitus of Vienne*, 209, where Shanzer and Wood pointed out that it is also unclear which Chilperic, either Gundobad's uncle or his brother, was named *Magister Utriusque Militiae* and *Patricius* in A.D. 474 and then

Eastern Emperor Leo had disagreed with Gundobad's imperial selection and sent Julius Nepos to Rome to take the throne by force. Gundobad did not meet Julius Nepos and instead was in the Burgundian territory, perhaps gathering soldiers or hoping to solidify his claims of inheritance against those of his brothers. Thus, with no real opposition, Nepos arrived in Italy, unseated Glycerius and was proclaimed Emperor at Rome on June 24, 474.[226]

Gundobad's activities in Rome as both *magister militum* and *patricius* exposed him to the Roman court. He was probably well educated, perhaps moreso than most of his contemporary barbarian kings (with the possible exception of the Ostrogoth King Theodoric) and he was familiar with imperial politics and the workings of Rome. This familiarity proved valuable in his later career as king of a nation of Burgundians and Romans.[227]

Burgundian King

After the death of King Gundioc, Burgundy,

---

continued to rule in Lyonss and Geneva. It is my belief that since Gundioc and Chilperic I assumed leadership of the Burgundians shortly after Chalons (A.D. 451), it seems plausible that the title of MVM was probably given to Gundobad's brother Chilperic II, who would have been close in age to his brother and more militarily active than a relatively old uncle, and thus a more likely candidate to mount a defense against Euric's Visigoths.

[226] Bury, *Roman Empire*, 1:405; Murray, *Merovingian Gaul*, 243; and Heather, "The Huns," 36.

[227] *Avitus of Vienne*, 15; and see , Michael Frassetto, ed., "Gundobad," in *Encyclopedia of Barbarian Europe: Society in Transformation* (Santa Barbara, Cal.: ABC Clio, 2003), 192-93, for a concise encapsulation of Gundobad's career.

according to Gregory of Tours, was divided among his four sons, with Chilperic II reigning at Lyons, Gundobad at Vienne, and Godegisel at Geneva while Godomar's capital is not known. Historians have come to believe that Gundobad divided the kingship, but not the physical kingdom, with his three brothers.[228] Under this system, Gundobad's brothers were also kings. They didn't share in the rule of the oldest brother who was high king and resided in his own capital, Lyons. The younger sons were given territories with urban residences in Geneva, Vienne and Valence. However, the younger sons did not actually divide up the realm for a split rule. It is possible that instead of ruling, they administered specific regions and collected the tax revenue generated in the region they administered. This configuration may have been influenced by the Huns, who the Burgundians sometimes emulated.[229]

Sidonius wrote two letters that shed light on some of the political machinations within Burgundy shortly after Julius Nepos took the throne. In the first, a

---

[228] Wolfram, *Germanic Peoples*, 253, noted that this was a uniquely Burgundian political system and was also mentioned in the *Niebelungenlied*; and Ian Wood, "Kings, Kingdoms and Consent," 21-22; and Barnwell, *Emperor, Prefects, & Kings*, 83. Given that Lyonss seems to have been the residence of the "primary" king, it would seem that Chilperic II may have been the eldest son of Gundioc. This is supported by the fact that it was Gundobad who went to Rome to make his name, a route that probably would not have been followed by the eldest son and heir but was commonly followed by second, or younger, sons. Also note that when Chilperic II died, Gundobad assumed his seat in Lyonss and was then regarded as the primary king among the Burgundians.

[229] Wolfram, *Germanic Peoples*, 257.

letter to his uncle Appolinaris, he related how Appolinaris's brother Thaumastus was worried for Appolinaris. As Sidonius wrote, "He is certain that the venomous tongues of certain villains have been secretly at work, whispering in the ear of the master of the soldiers, the ever-victorious Chilperic, that it was chiefly your doing that the town of Vaison was won over to the side of the new emperor."[230] That Chilperic II would be upset at any that supported the rival to his kinsman's choice for emperor was understandable. Thus, if Chilperic II believed these rumors, Appolinaris had much to fear.[231]

Sidonius assured Apollinaris that he would be his advocate and investigate the charges. In a subsequent letter to Thaumastus, Sidonius related that he had discovered who the rumor mongers were and bemoaned the fact that Apollinaris was in a dangerous situation. However, Sidonius also provided some hope to Thaumastus. In an allegorical passage, he praised Chilperic II's wife:

> But the chief consolation in our troubles is this: our Lucumo is restrained by his Tanaquil. With a timely and witty word, she rids her husband's ears of the poisonous tales instilled there by

---

[230] Sidonius, in Murray, *Merovingian Gaul*, 243.

[231] More importantly, this could be taken as evidence that the relationship between Chilperic II and Gundobad was not one in which fratricide would be the ultimate outcome.

whisperers. You should know that up till now it has been her doing that the mind of our common patron has not been poisoned against the well-being of our brothers by these younger Cibyrates; God willing, that will never happen while the present power rules a Lyonese Germania, and our present Agrippina exerts

her moderating influence on her and our Germanicus.[232]

Sidonius held this unnamed queen in high regard. His account of her advising her husband is almost all that is known about Chilperic II's wife.

The Burgundians were politically and militarily strong prior to the emergence of Euric at the head of the Visigoths. Yet, with his emergence and the nearly simultaneous establishment of another Gothic kingdom in Italy, they sought imperial assurances and support. In A.D. 474, the Burgundians and the Empire renewed their old treaties and the Burgundian kings were allowed to re-assume Roman military offices.[233] Gundobad most likely had a large part to play in these negotiations.

---

[232] Sidonius, in Murray, *Merovingian Gaul*, 244. Obviously, Lucumo/Tanaquil and Germanicus/Agrippina are allusions to Chilperic II and his wife. The first were a legendary king and queen of Rome and the second were involved in Roman politics and intrigue c. A.D. 20. The Cibyrates were two brothers who helped Verres, a governor of Sicily, plunder his province in 73-30 B.C.

[233] Wolfram, *Germanic Peoples*, 221.

In the Auvergne, up until around A.D. 475, the Burgundians supported the efforts of the Gallic senators to oppose Euric. They were distracted by conflict with the Alamanni over the Langres, Besançon and the Jura, which they successfully gained. Thus, part of Lugdunensis I and all of Maxima Sequanorum fell into their hands. During this time, Euric persisted in his attempts to obtain the rich country of Auvergne, which held out for four years. Perhaps as a result of the relative inattention of the Burgundians, the Auvergne was eventually ceded to him as part of a peace agreement with Julius Nepos in A.D. 475. The agreement greatly strengthened the Goths, who had already conquered Spain and the Aquitaine. The peace lasted for a year, then Euric seized Arles and Marseilles. Anthemius's successor, Zeno, could not change the situation and conceded southern Provence to the Goths. The Burgundians, wary of their dangerous neighbor, also made peace with Euric.[234]

From A.D. 474, when he left Rome, until A.D. 490, little, if anything, is known of Gundobad's actions, though it is not too far of a stretch to assume that he took some part in the battles against the Goths and also in negotiations with both Rome and Constantinople. However, in A.D. 490, Gundobad took advantage of the conflict in Italy between Odovacar and Theodoric the Ostrogoth, and sent an army into northern Italy to pillage the countryside. He may have done so in support

---

[234] Dill, *Roman Society*, 83; Jordanes, *Goths*, 36-8; Bury, *Roman Empire*, 1:342-3; and Wolfram, *Germanic Peoples*, 252.

of Odovacar,[235] he may have been playing the vulture, or he may have been wary of being caught between two Goth kingdoms and hoped a preemptive strike would weaken Theodoric to prevent such a situation.[236]

He also may have had more legal matters in mind, too, as he would later claim that his actions had been to gain compensation at the expense of the Ligurians for the violation of a treaty on the part of one of their rulers.[237] Gundobad pillaged the countryside and took Ligurian captives and, his goal accomplished, returned to his lands before Theodoric could muster a force to confront him. Shortly thereafter, Theodoric sent an embassy to parley for the return of hostages. Bishop Epiphanius was head of this diplomatic group and was accompanied by Ennodius, who wrote:

> Liguria had been devastated by the Burgundians; King Gundobad had carried thousands into captivity, and no husbandmen were left to till the soil and tend the vineyards. Theodoric was prepared to ransom the captives, and he charged Epiphanius with the office of persuading the Burgundian king to release them. The bishop, notwithstanding his infirm age, undertook the cold and

---

[235] Ibid., 253.

[236] Ennodius *Opera*, ed. Hartel, (1882), 276, 369, (*Hist. Misc.* 15.16) in Bury, *Roman Empire*, 1:424-5; and Bury, *Invasion of Europe*, 181.

[237] Wolfram, *Germanic Peoples*, 253.

difficult journey over the Alps in March (A.D. 494), and was received by Gundobad at Lyons. To the arguments and prayers of the envoy, Gundobad, who was an excellent speaker, replied with the frank and cynical assertion that war permits and justifies everything which is unlawful in peace. 'War ignores the bridle of moderation which you, as a Christian luminary, teach. It is a fixed principle with belligerents that whatever is not lawful is lawful when they are fighting. The object of war is to cut up your opponent's strength at the roots.' He went on to say that a peace had now been concluded — it had been sealed by the betrothal of a daughter of Theodoric to Gundobad's son Sigismund — and that if the bishop and his companions would return to their homes he would consider what it were best to do in the interests of his soul and his kingdom. Epiphanius had gained his cause. Gundobad set free all prisoners who were in his own hands, without charge, and those who were the slaves of private persons were ransomed. More than six thousand were restored to Italy.[238]

---

[238] Ennodius, *Opera*, in Bury, *Roman Empire*, 1:427.

What is clear is that, by this time, it seems Gundobad was the preeminent king among the Burgundians. Theodoric had to contend with four chief powers; the Visigoths, the Burgundians, the Franks, and the Vandals. As such, he used his female relatives as agents of political alliances. As alluded to in the above passage, Theodoric gave one daughter Ostrogotho-Areagni to Gundobad's son, Sigismund, and another, Thiudogotho to the Visigothic king Alaric II. He himself married Audofleda, sister of the Frankish king Clovis. There is no chronology of the marriages, though it is probable that the marriages of Theodoric and Clovis took place before those of Theodoric's daughters. The marriage between Sigismund and Ostrogotho was probably formalized by A.D. 496 and occurred no later than A.D. 497. With these marriages, Theodoric hoped that close family ties with other barbarian powers would both maintain peace in Western Europe and secure his own position in Italy.[239] Gundobad also saw the diplomatic benefits of royal marriage and arranged for his niece, Clotilda, to marry the Frank king, Clovis.

---

[239] Jordanes, *Goths*, 46; Wolfram, *Germanic Peoples*, 254; and Bury, *Roman Empire*, 2:153, 1:461-62, also noted that Theodoric additionally gave gifts to Gundobad, including a sun-dial, a water-clock, and a celestial globe.

CHAPTER 7
CLOTILDA AND CLOVIS
(474 A.D. TO 501 A.D.)

Chilperic II's daughter Clotilda was born at Lyons around A.D. 474. She had a younger sister named Sedeluba, or Chrona (sometimes Chroma), and both were educated as Christians, probably under the guidance their mother, who was most likely Roman Catholic. They were probably familiar with the saints of Lyons, such as the slave martyr Saint Blandina. They were also brought up in the busy court of Chilperic II, which was probably frequented by many Catholic bishops and other luminaries. These included Sidonius, who was a regular visitor and the Catholic bishops Avitus of Vienne and Patiens of Lyons.[240] That she was surrounded by such religious personages as Avitus and Patiens has lead some to theorize that she was undoubtedly much influenced by them in the faith.[241]

---

[240] Godefroid Kurth, *Saint Clotilda*, trans. V.M. Crawford with a preface by G. Tyrell (London: Duckworth & Co., 1898), 21.

[241] See Kurth, *Saint Clotilda*, 22, "It was a special privilege for Clotilda to be able to study the Catholic Church through such representative ecclesiastics, and we should bear in mind the influence they doubtless exercised over her."

Thus, it is widely accepted that Clotilda's mother, and perhaps her father, were Catholic.[242] Clotilda's mother was mentioned by Sidonius who sang her praises,[243] and compared her to Tanaquil and Agrippina, "each of which recalls the influence exercised by a noble-hearted woman over her husband."[244]

Chilperic II probably died around A.D. 490 and his daughters were sent to the court of Godegisel in Geneva when Gundobad took the throne at Lyons.[245] The death of Chilperic II, as described by Gregory of Tours, has spawned a debate among historians that has filled volumes. According to Gregory, "Gundobad killed his brother Chilperic and drowned Chilperic's wife after tying a stone round her neck. He drove Chilperic's two daughters into exile: the elder, whose name was Chroma, became a religious, and the younger was called Clotild[a]."[246] Some believe the sisters went to Geneva because Godegisel was Catholic, while Gundobad was an Arian.[247] In Geneva, Clotilda became a pious Christian and she and her sister performed charitable deeds.

---

[242] *Avitus of Vienne*, 209.

[243] Kurth, *Saint Clotilda*, 20, stated that while Sidonius was "addicted to hyperbole," the compliments he gave to the wife of Chilperic II were probably not those of a cloying sycophant. "Sidonius had no affection for the Burgundians, and did not owe allegiance to Chilperic."

[244] Kurth, *Saint Clotilda*, 20.

[245] If this is so, it is possible that Chilperic II was the eldest, and when he died, Gundobad assumed the throne as the preeminent king among his remaining brothers.

[246] Gregory of Tours, *The History of the Franks*, 141; see James, *The Origins of France*, 23, for the observation that "Gregory himself is on the whole hostile to Gundobad."

[247] Kurth, *Saint Clotilda*, 22-23.

According to Fredegarius, Sedeluba (Chroma) founded the Church of St Victor in the outskirts of Geneva[248] and disappeared from the pages of history. Clotilda was also pious, she was said to have washed the feet of the poor,[249] however, unlike her sister, Clotilda's fate was not a nunnery. She had a still larger role to play for the Church.

The Marriage of Clotilda and Clovis

According to Gregory, Clovis had envoys in Burgundy who reported back to him about the beautiful and intelligent princess Clotilda. He sent messengers to Gundobad and asked for her hand in marriage. Afraid to refuse the wishes of a powerful, neighboring king, Gundobad acceded and entrusted Clotilda to Clovis' envoys. They took her back to Clovis, who was pleased by the sight of Clotilda and married her.[250] The Fredegarius account is more detailed, though not necessarily more accurate. According to this version of the story, Clotilda and her sister were doing charitable work and were secluded and hidden from Clovis' men. Eventually, Clovis sent a trusted Roman retainer named Aurelian, disguised as a beggar, to find Clotilda. Once

---

[248] Fredegarus, IV. 22, in Kurth, *Saint Clotilda*, 24.

[249] Fredegarus, III. 18, in Kurth, *Saint Clotilda*, 24.

[250] Gregory of Tours, *The History of the Franks*, 140-41; and *Avitus of Vienne*, 20, in which Shanzer and Wood theorized that "at some point, probably after his return to power in 500, [Gundobad] may have proposed a marriage between his own daughter and Clovis. Her death, however, which is recorded by Avitus, may well have led to the substitution of Gundobad's niece, [Clotilda], the daughter of [Chilperic] , as a bride for the Frankish king." This was based on a close reading of Avitus, Episula 5.

Aurelian found her, he gave her Clovis' ring as a show of faith. Clotilda was overjoyed and gave Aurelian her own ring to return to Clovis, telling him to have Clovis ask Gundobad for permission to marry her. She urged haste for fear that a counselor to her uncle, Aridius, would arrive from Constantinople and dissuade Gundobad from allowing the marriage.[251]

Gundobad, apparently afraid of Frankish power, agreed to the union and Clovis and Clotilda were formally betrothed at Chalon-sur-Sâone, in A.D. 493. She began her journey to her new kingdom in a treasure-filled carriage guarded by Frankish warriors. While traveling, she heard that Aridius returned to Gundobad's court. Fearing pursuit, she ordered the Franks to put her on horseback to speed her travel. Meanwhile, Aridius had warned Gundobad of the peril of a marriage between Clovis and Clotilda, claiming she might prevail upon him to avenge the death of her father and brothers, which had been ordered by Gundobad. Gundobad sent a party of Burgundian warriors to abduct Clotilda, but her foresight had saved her and she had already reached the border of the Frankish kingdom. Once safe, she ordered the surrounding countryside to be ravaged by her escort and then gave thanks to God because her revenge had thus begun.[252]

The Gregory and Fredegarius accounts portrayed

---

[251] Fredegarius. *Historia Francorum Epitomata*. Ed. Migne, lxxi and *M.G.H. R. Merov. Ii.* (1888) 89 ff., ed. Krusch. (iii, 18-19) in Dill, *Roman Society*, 83-84.

[252] Ibid., 84.

Gundobad in an unflattering light, but the truth may have been different than that put forth by these Merovingian propagandists.[253] Many have continued to accept these accounts of Clotilda and the events surrounding her while she lived in Burgundy, but a few have not. That Clovis probably married her in the early 490's and that she was the niece of King Gundobad is accepted. However, the story, or legend, of Gundobad's murder of Chilperic II and Clotilda's subsequent desire for revenge grew up about a generation after the marriage of Clovis and Clotilda. Some historians have

---

[253] The debate regarding the credibility of the accounts of Gregory of Tours has encompassed nearly as many years as did the duration of the Burgundian Kingdom in Gaul. For one of the earlier (at least in modern times) arguments against Gregory's story, see Kurth, *Saint Clotilda*, 31-32. Kurth examined Gregory's own sources and concluded that he relied too much on legend, which he uncritically used to fill in gaps in his otherwise historical record; and I.N. Wood, "Continuity or calamity?: the constraints of literary models," in *Fifth-century Gaul: a crisis of identity?*, ed. Drinkwater and Elton, 13, who remarked that "the account of fifth-century Gaul offered by Gregory in his Histories is intended, on the one hand, to denigrate the Arian Goths and Burgundians, and, on the other, to elevate the Franks and their king, the Catholic convert, Clovis."; Wallace-Hadrill, *The Long-Haired Kings*, 63, who unequivocally stated that Gregory's hero is Clovis, and Gregory placed Clovis' conversion too early to make it appear as if all of Clovis' great deeds were done as a Catholic. Wallace-Hadrill's chapter, "The Work of Gregory of Tours in the Light of Modern Research," 49-70, in *The Long-Haired Kings*, is informative on the subject Gregory's work, point of view and motivation; and see Ian Wood, *The Merovingian Kingdoms*, 42, for the statement that, "Gregory's account of Clovis seems to be more concerned to create the image of a catholic king against whom his successors could be assessed, than with any desire to provide an accurate account of the reign. In order to understand Clovis within the context of the late fifth and early sixth centuries it is necessary to emphasize the contemporary evidence, and to treat Gregory, as far as possible, as a secondary source."

been critical of its widespread acceptance as historical fact. They have contended that the story threw "a shadow over the character of Clotilda, and a still darker shadow over the character of King Gundobad"[254] and maintained that the "the very basis of [the story] is entirely fictitious."[255] These historians have relied on a textual criticism of both Gregory and Fredegarius as well as other sources that mention Clotilda, including the Saint's Lives.[256]

---

[254] Kurth, "St. Clotilda," in *Catholic Encyclopedia*, 1908 ed.; also see Randers-Pehrson, *Barbarians and Romans*, 263, in which it was explained some of the historiographical problems with the story of Clovis. First is the chronological problem, "which is wellnigh hopeless." It has been the subject of scholarly debate for decades. "What confidence can be placed in judgements that sometimes must be based on the tense of a verb in a manuscript corrupted by copyists whose knowledge of Latin was admittedly faulty?" The second problem is on the primary source, Gregory of Tours. He "was a honest man, but he was possessed with a burning desire to prove that Clovis, from a very early time in his extraordinary career, had been the champion of true Christianity." She also noted that most agree Gregory placed Clovis's conversion too early so that all of his campaigns would be deemed victories for the Church. The third problem is the anachronistic belief that Clovis sought to create a French nation. "In reality, if we read closely, he was a greedy opportunist who seized upon whatever chances arose in the flux of any given critical situation." The first two problems seem viable while the last may be a bit too cynical for most. Though it may also be true!

[255] Bury, *Invasion of Europe*, 237.

[256] Jane Tibbetts Schulenburg, *Forgetful of Their Sex: Female Sanctity and Society ca. 500-1100* (Chicago: University of Chicago Press, 1998), 17-18, 182, warned that, while hagiography often provided the only source of information for medieval women, it is important to note that most hagiographers were less historians than saint propagandists. This does not necessarily exclude Saints Lives as valuable historical sources, she continued, but historians must be aware of the motivation of the hagiographer. However, later in the work, Schulenburg is far more

Some have held that Clotilda had no reason to avenge her father's death by Gundobad because Gundobad didn't commit the murders. They cited as proof a letter written by Bishop Avitus of Vienne to console Gundobad on the death of a daughter.[257] Within this letter, Avitus wrote that, "[i]n the past, with ineffable tender-heartedness, you mourned the deaths of your brothers."[258] Accordingly, the brother mentioned was not Godegisel who later fought Gundobad and died, so it must have referred to Chilperic II. Another alternative may have been that the unnamed brother was the mysterious Godomar, who was barely

---

accepting of the account as given in the *Liber Historiae Francorum*, which she used to conclude that Clotilda was a woman who was active in determining her own destiny, "Considering that Gundobad had killed her parents and exiled her sister, and continued to espouse Arianism, Clotilda was no doubt anxious to escape from his court and to start a new life."; for a similar warning against the propagandistic quality of Saints' Lives, see Wood, "Continuity or calamity?," 15; and Wallace-Hadrill, *The Long-Haired Kings*, 131, who described that Clotilda urged her sons to attack Gundobad's as part of a "blood feud," and note 3 for his succinct statement that "Some historians look upon the story as essentially a myth. I do not know why."; finally, see Kurth, *Saint Clotilda*, 133, who believed that both Fredegarus and the monk of St Denis, who wrote the *Liber Historiae* were even less critical of their sources than Gregory. Kurth also offered a defense of the hagiographers (141) when he wrote "on this occasion at least hagiography can defend the legitimacy of its traditions in the name of science, while on the other hand we have the amusing spectacle of rationalistic learning, engaged in angry argument against the conclusions of the critical methods. Can it be true that in the estimation of certain historians the legends which glorify the saints are the only ones to be struck out, while those that calumniate them are to be preserved with pious care?"

[257] *Avitus of Vienne*, Epistula 5, 210-12.
[258] Ibid., 210.

mentioned in the sources. Thus, Avitus' letter seemed to absolve Gundobad of the murder of Chilperic II.[259]

Another piece of evidence that has often been cited was that the woman believed to have been Clotilda's mother, Caretena, had an epitaph that survived in a church in Lyons. On it, her name was clearly visible as Caretena, and it stated that she died in A.D. 506, "full of days," and years after her Clotilda's marriage. This has been held as proof that Clotilda's mother was not thrown down the well as told by Gregory and that she survived for quite some time after her purported murder. However, this argument has more recently been convincingly debunked as current scholarship holds that Caretena was, in fact, Gundobad's, not Chilperic II's, wife.[260]

Regardless of the lively ongoing debate, the political factors that influenced the marriage have been

---

[259] *Avitus of Vienne*, Epistula 5, 210; also see Bury, *Invasion of Europe*, 237; Kurth, *Saint Clotilda*, 139; Wolfram, *Germanic Peoples*, 253, noted that, "It is likely that both Godomar and Chilperic II—the father of Clotild[a], the future wife of Clovis—died natural deaths around 490." These are but a few who doubted that Gundobad killed his brother.

[260] Bury, *Invasion of Europe*, 237; Kurth, *Saint Clotilda*, 139; and especially *Avitus of Vienne*, 209, note 2, for the comment, based on close scrutiny of PLRE 2, that "What is certainly wrong is the identification of Chilperic II's wife as Caretena: she was unquestionably the wife of Gundobad."; and Schulenburg, *Forgetful of Their Sex*, 181, who pointed out that the exact relation of Caretena to Clotilda is subject to debate and also asserted that Clotilda stayed with Gundobad while her sister became a nun. No one seems to have considered the possibility that even in late antiquity it was not unkown for people to travel between cities! In other words, it's possible Clotilda spent time in both locales.

recognized. There may have been two sides in the kingdom of Burgundy, one that favored an alliance with the Franks, led by Godegisel, and another that mistrusted such an alliance, led by Gundobad. Clotilda had been living at Geneva, the capital of her uncle Godegisel, who, as will be shown, made a secret pact with Clovis. Thus, that Clotilda was Catholic was known to Clovis beforehand and was probably considered to be a desirable condition. "Pious intrigue" was probably partly influential in matching a Catholic princess with the king of the pagan Franks.

Since the Burgundians were known Arians, as were all of the other barbarian tribes at the time, was it a coincidence that Clovis chose a Catholic Burgundian princess from this particular tribe? However, though the Burgundians were Arian, they also seemed more tolerant of their Catholic subjects than the Vandals and Visigoths, and some of Gundobad's closest advisors, such as Patiens and Avitus, were Catholic bishops. Though he may have not been Christian himself, it is probable that Clovis realized the political benefits of having a Catholic wife, especially one related to, at the time, a strong Arian kingdom that was also sympathetic to Catholics. The Burgundians also realized the importance of political marriages, as when Gundobad married his son to Theodoric's daughter. For Clovis though, a marriage to Clotilda was more important for the ties it would strengthen to the dominant Roman Catholic Church than with those of the Burgundian kingdom.

Whether Gregory's or Fredegarius' accounts of Clotilda's flight from the Burgundian kingdom to meet her betrothed are believable or not, what has been generally accepted is that the marriage was arranged at Chalon-sur-Sâone and that Clovis met her at Villery, south of Troyes, and accompanied her to Soissons for the wedding. A poem written describing the ceremony replaced the historical facts as the historical record.[261] "In this way legend at an early date took the place of historical fact, and, during many centuries, all that was best known of the life of Clotilda was that which never really occurred."[262]

Clotilda and Clovis lived first in Soissons, in the residence of the Roman Governor located north of the town. Yet, while this was home, Clotilda traveled much, for the Merovingian kings had no real capital city, and were often guests in the estate of some wealthy aristocrat who could afford to house and feed the retinue of the Frankish king. How often Clotilda accompanied Clovis, or whether she stayed in Soissons is unknown.[263]

Clotilda and the Conversion of Clovis

Some believe marriage of Clovis and Clotilda was strong and that it must have encouraged marital fidelity because there is no evidence that Clovis begat any

---

[261] Kurth, *Saint Clotilda*, 28, 30.
[262] Ibid., 30.
[263] Kurth, *Saint Clotilda*, 31-2, assumed Clotilda traveled with Clovis throughout his domain.

illegitimate offspring after their marriage. No illegitimate heir surfaced in the years of conflict between the sons of Clovis, which tends to support and confirm that Theuderic was Clovis's only illegitimate son. Clovis was certainly patient with his proselytizing wife and her persistent attempts to sway him to Christianity.[264] "It is obvious that she must have enjoyed considerable ascendancy over his mind in order to have repeatedly urged so great a sacrifice without fear of violent refusal."[265]

While there has been much written about Clovis's battlefield epiphany, Clotilda undoubtedly laid the groundwork.[266] Further, it's "the 'Christ of Clotilda' whom Clovis invokes" and "neither St. [Remigius] nor other members of the official church hierarchy were similarly awarded this type of prominence."[267] There

---

[264] Kurth, *Saint Clotilda*, 32; and Schulenburg, *Forgetful of Their Sex,* 184.

[265] Kurth, *Saint Clotilda*, 32.

[266] Wallace-Hadrill, *The Long-Haired Kings*, 169, "The pattern is familiar. Defeat stares him in the face and his gods have deserted him; his thoughts turn to his wife's god, to whom he prays in his heart for victory; and victory is his. Like Constantine in a similar predicament, Clovis knows that he must throw in his lot with the new god." Also see note 3: "The parallel with the battle of the Milvian Bridge does not disprove the later story. His wife and St Remigius were there to remind Clovis of Constantine, if he needed reminding."; and Wood, *The Merovingian Kingdoms*, 44, noted that Avitus made no mention of Clotilda's role in converting Clovis, nor of a battlefield conversion, but credits Clovis for finding his own way.

[267] Schulenburg, *Forgetful of Their Sex,* 185-86; also see Wallace-Hadrill, *The Long-Haired Kings*, 166-67, for the assertion that while Clovis showed goodwill to the Catholic bishops by his marriage to Clotilda, his marriage did not prompt his conversion, despite the efforts of his wife and Bishop Remigius.

was also risk for Clovis in deciding to convert. The majority of the Franks were pagan or Arian and for Clovis to maintain his power over the Franks, his bodyguard would also have agreed to convert or they would have disbanded and eliminated Clovis's power base. Clovis had doubts as to whether they would join him and called a meeting to inform them of his intention. They all agreed to be converted with their king. Thus, around 3,000 of his warriors, (though this may be an exaggerated number) were baptized with him.[268] "His conversion, therefore, implied great risk and required great courage."[269]

---

[268] Bury, *Invasion of Europe*, 241; Dill, *Roman Society*, 83-84, 89; and Jeremiah O'Sullivan and John F. Burns, *Medieval Europe* (New York: F.S. Crofts & Co., 1943), 164, concurred with Dill that Clovis did risk losing his power base by converting; Kurth, *Saint Clotilda*, 48-49, believed that the average Frank cared not what the religion of his ruler was, but this was not so for the bodyguard, which was "bound to the king by a pledge of honour, was associated in all his acts and shared in his good and evil fortunes...they shared in all his personal interests, in his friendships and enmities, and his Gods were their Gods. What would become of this intimate communion of views and sentiments when Clovis passed from the service of Wodin to the service of Christ?"

[269] O'Sullivan and Burns, *Medieval Europe*, 164; also see Wallace-Hadrill, *The Long-Haired Kings*, 169-70, which theorized that Clovis's conversion wasn't "total" but more the acceptance of another god "to his people's pantheon, perhaps in a commanding position." Still, this is different than baptism and "officially" accepting no other gods but the Christian. This last was probably made easier by the "pantheon" of saints. "But even adhesion calls for conviction of right, and it is no belittlement of Clovis' act to term it a political decision, taken after weighing Frankish pagan conservatism against the assured approval of the Gallo-Romans." Perhaps the Gallo-Roman episcopate had finally demanded conversion, or Clovis had thought that the Empire would actively support him against the Goths. "Without Tolbiac [the battle with the Alamans], the proof would

There are other arguments made on behalf of the influence wielded by Clotilda. A strong queen could take advantage of the vague definition of her role in the early middle ages. Her presence at the royal court and position as mother to royal heirs gave her access to her husband, his advisers and the royal treasury. At the death of Clovis, Clotilda was probably a very politically influential figure in the kingdom, given the young age of her children and the attachments in court she had no doubt made, including the significant support of the Catholic bishops, such as Remigius.[270]

She would need these contacts and their support, and possibly that of her Burgundian relatives, over the next few years. Clovis left behind four sons, but only three were sons of Clotilda. The eldest son, Theuderic, was much older than his half-brothers and even had a son of his own, Theudebert. He was probably in a politically strong position, with military victories and his own loyal warriors, and was a severe threat to the welfare of Clotilda and her sons. Assuming that a mother would be predisposed to guarantee the welfare of her children, it is plausible to propose that a political compromise was reached between she and Theuderic.[271]

---

have been lacking that the Christian god gave victory over other Germans."

[270] Ian Wood, "Kings, Kingdoms and Consent," 6, 26; and Janet Nelson, "Queens as Jezebels: The careers of Brunhild and Balthild in Merovingian History," in *Medieval Women. Dedicated and presented to Professor Rosalind M.T. Hill on the occasion of her seventieth birthday*, ed. D. Baker (Oxford, 1978), 31-77, in Elisabeth van Houts, "The State of Research: Women in Medieval History and Literature," *Journal of Medieval History* 20 (1994), 287.

[271] Wood, "Kings, Kingdoms and Consent," 26.

As well as church support, Clotilda may have also called on her relationship with her Burgundian relatives to add muscle to the negotiations. It seems doubtful that Theuderic could be checked solely by the officials of a religion to which he had but recently converted, if he did at all. The bishops and the aristocrats were probably instrumental in defining the division of the Frankish kingdom, which "followed the lines of the old Roman *civitas* boundaries. The experts here were the bishops and the Gallo-Roman aristocracy. The division is inconceivable without their approval."[272] Finally, evidence points to the land division of A.D. 511 between Clotilda's sons and Theuderic as the first such splitting of inheritance. Regardless of the particulars, it can be inferred that Clotilda was successful in preserving the birthright, and survival, of her sons.[273]

---

[272] Wood, "Kings, Kingdoms and Consent," 26, admitted that the formulation of such negotiations is purely speculative, "but it seems plausible to suggest" that the division was a "political compromise" not "tradition."; and Katharine Scherman, *The Birth of France: Warriors, Bishops and Long-Haired Kings* (New York: Random House, 1987), 135, who believed that Clotilda "in an attempt to foster harmony, designated as capitals of the four kingdoms cities in a near arc around Paris ....Anticipating the predictable clashes of her hotheaded, only semicivilzed sons, it was likely that she was also the one who persuaded them to respect Paris as neutral territory."

[273] Wood, "Kings, Kingdoms and Consent," 11, argued further that Childebert and Chlothar would later have to make a similar compromise with their nephew Theudebert (son of Theuderic, and perhaps older than his uncles) who had the support of many within the kingdom. This seems to have created a "tradition" of land partition between heirs. "If this is so, what looks to us like Frankish tradition may only have been formed by the political compromises of the first half of the sixth century. One result of

Clotilda, Clovis and the Burgundian Civil War

Around A.D. 500, Gundobad and Godegisel ruled together in Burgundy, though Gundobad was probably the arch-king while Godegisel was his subordinate, probably ruling only the territory around Geneva more directly.[274] The fate of their brother Godomar was not recorded. The cause of their rivalry is unknown, and it appears they had peacefully coexisted for some time. That Godigisel was the aggressor in the event was evident. Perhaps sibling rivalry or Godigisel's jealousy over the position and fame of his older brother, or resentment over the partitioning of the kingdom whereby Gundobad had received most of Chilperic I's former lands, had prompted Godigisel to approach Clovis about an alliance against his brother. Clovis had been winning great victories against other barbarian tribes and Godegisel heard of these and sent ambassadors to him asking for aid in attacking Gundobad.[275] In exchange, Godegisel offered tribute at a rate determined by Clovis.

Clovis accepted the offer, and there have been many theories as to why he did. Perhaps he did it simply based on loyalty to his wife's former guardian. Godegisel had essentially been Clotilda's foster father and may have been a Catholic himself.[276] Additionally, as

---

such a suggestion must be that in 511 [Clotilda] could not have been certain that her sons, young as they were, would survive."

[274] Wood, "Kings, Kingdoms and Consent," 21-22.

[275] Kurth, *Saint Clotilda*, 59-60.

[276] Kurth, *Saint Clotilda*, 60, who also relied on Pardessus, *Diplomata*, vol.I., 156, to observe, "We know at least that in conjunction with his wife

Godigisel was less powerful than Gundobad, he was less of a threat to Clovis, who probably could not have easily passed up an opportunity to severely weaken, if not destroy, a dangerous rival. Some assumed that Clotilda, if forced to choose, probably would have sided with the uncle under whose care she had been given, "[b]ut, at the same time, while coming to the help of the one, she had no wish to make relentless war on the other."[277] Similar to this, others have said that the simple fact of being related to the Burgundians was enough motivation for Clovis to get involved.[278] Others contended that Clovis sought to kill Gundobad to avenge the murder of his wife's parents. Yet, even when he had such a chance, he ultimately did not exact said revenge.[279]

Theodelinda, he built the monastery of St. Peter at Lyonss."

[277] Kurth, *Saint Clotilda*, 61, believed Clotilda saw Clovis's intervention as a chance to save Godigisel rather than to destroy Gundobad.

[278] Wallace-Hadrill, *The Long-Haired Kings*, 167, asserted that Clovis involved himself in the internal affairs of Burgundy because his wife was a Burgundian, he essentially married into it. "It was the fact of kinship, not of his wife's Catholicism....Clovis marched into Burgundy at the invitation of one of his kinsmen by marriage, Godigisel, caring little where it might lead."

[279] James, *The Franks*, 85-86, who theorized that though Clovis could have sought vengeance on behalf of his wife, "if he was a more cynical politician than Gregory allows," then the story of Gundobad murdering Clotilda's parents "served the Franks as useful propaganda for many years."; Scherman, *The Birth of France*, 115, stated there was no direct evidence that Clotilda encouraged Clovis in his conquest of Burgundy because "the Christian bias of the chroniclers" saw the "motive of revenge" as "immoral."; to points similar to this, Kurth, *Saint Clotilda*, viii, had observed, "To a bloody-minded and barbarous people, in a state of spiritual infancy, how could Clotilda, the great and the good, lack any element necessary to their crude ideal; how could she be otherwise than vengeful, if vengeance were a point of honour, and if to forgive were weakness and

Some at least partly attributed Clovis's interest in the Burgundian civil war as a sort of thanks to his wife for helping to convert him, implying that Clovis thought it would be appropriate to fight Arians.[280] Others have countered that, though the conversion of Clovis and his Franks helped him to consolidate power, there can be no doubt that had they been Arian, they would have still attacked the Burgundians and Visigoths "in accord with their definite policy of expansion, pursued by Clovis even before his conversion."[281] Some believed that more earthly, and immediate, circumstances motivated Clovis. After Clovis had captured Soissons and all of her riches, he was aware that his warriors would expect continued success and booty. A civil war would have seemed a perfect opportunity to satisfy his warriors.[282]

No matter how or why Clovis intervened, he moved to attack Gundobad, who was forewarned of Clovis' movements but unaware of his brother's treachery. He sent for Godegisel's aid to ward off the Frank attack and was assured of Godegisel's assistance. The three kings met on the field of battle, near Dijon, and the battle joined on the river Ouche. Godegisel

---

cowardice? As surely as the mind of childhood has got its stereotyped king and queen and prince, ever crowned in high state and radiant with gold, so surely has the childlike multitude certain moulds into which every hero or saint must be pressed unless the public imagination is to be pained and shocked."

[280] Wolfram, *Germanic Peoples*, 254.

[281] O'Sullivan and Burns, *Medieval Europe*, 163.

[282] Randers-Pehrson, *Barbarians and Romans*, 263. This may also point to the possibility that Clovis could have approached Godigisel about a joint attack on Gundobad.

united his forces with Clovis' to crush the army of Gundobad, who fled when he saw he had been betrayed and followed the Rhône to the city of Avignon where he gathered reinforcements. Godegisel promised to hand part of his kingdom over to Clovis and went home to Vienne to celebrate his victory. Meanwhile, Clovis moved to attack Avignon and remove Gundobad.[283]

According to Gregory of Tours, Gundobad heard of these dire plans and was afraid.[284] He turned again to his wise advisor Aridius who concocted a plan of action.[285] In short, Aridius pretended to play the part of

---

[283] *Marius of Avenches* in Murray, *Merovingian Gaul*, 102, mentioned "the deceitful machinations of Godegisel against his brother Gundobad. In the battle Godegisel along with his followers fought alongside the Franks against his brother Gundobad. After Gundobad fled, Godegisel obtained his brother's kingdom for a little while, and Gundobad took refuge in Avignon."; and Wood, "Continuity or calamity?," 14-15, reminded that the fifth-century chronicles also pose problems for historical interpretation. "By the inclusion and omission of material, by grouping events and by placing them in particular years, a chronicler could embark on an interpretation of his period every bit as contrived as that of Gregory, and all the more misleading, because the literary form may be thought of as not being open to rhetorical abuse."

[284] Gregory of Tours, *The History of the Franks*, 145-47, provides the basis for this paragraph.

[285] *Avitus of Vienne*, 328-29, Epistula 50, is a correspondence between Avitus and a *dux* named Arigius. Some have identified Arigius as the Aridius mentioned in the story. The historical Arigius was having a new church dedicated and Avitus had to decline an invitation because of the Feast of St. Peter, important to the church of Vienne. The identification of these two men being the same individual is based on this passage from Epistula 50: "Because, unlike a bride, who had to be joined in whatever way to such a husband, as she was promised, even though cult-vessels were badly needed, nonetheless it was right to fear the weapons of the plunderers more. Therefore, after you had given due consideration to all the circumstances, brave man as you are, you changed the nature of your

a turncoat. Clovis's army had surrounded the city, so Aridius approached the lines of Clovis's army in his guise of a traitor. He won the confidence of Clovis, apparently because his reputation as a man of knowledge preceded him, and soon became a trusted advisor. Eventually, Aridius convinced Clovis that more profit was to be had from exacting tribute from Gundobad than from ravaging the surrounding lands while laying siege to a nearly impenetrable town. Clovis agreed to the plan to offer such a proposal to Gundobad and sent his army home. Gundobad agreed to Clovis's proposal, paid tribute for the current year and promised to do so in the future.

Some believed Clovis had no desire to destroy Gundobad, and was happy to only weaken him sufficiently. They trace this back to the influence of Clotilda and proposed that Clotilda acted as an ambassador between Clovis and Gundobad.[286] Further, if Clotilda's aim was to keep both of her uncles alive, then the fact that Clovis left five or six thousand men

---

steadfastness, and setting aside the boldness of your secular office of Dux, in which you are particularly skilled, you overcame, through your fear, whatever danger from the enemy was imminent. Therefore let everyone who sees the occasion for happiness before our eyes, praise your haste in the past. Safety snatched from adversity was appropriate to your arrangements. It was right that we first gain possession of what it had been your pleasure to adorn in this fashion." I think too much is being read into this and that Avitus is using allegory to describe the difficulties that this Arigius had in getting a church built, furnished and completed.

[286] Kurth, *Saint Clotilda*, 64-66. This of course assumed that she would have had no reason to desire the death of her uncle, Gundobad, in the first place.

with Godegisel before leaving for home could be viewed as an attempt to equalize the forces of Gundobad and Godigisel to prevent more fighting. Thus, from these circumstances, it could be construed that, because Clovis returned home without having completely vanquished his opponent, his people, unused to such "Frankish moderation," could not conceive of such an outcome. As a result, they (and later chroniclers) came to believe that what had really occurred was that their king, "in an excess of generous loyalty, had allowed himself to be tricked by the Burgundians."[287]   Rather than Clovis showing mercy to a relative at the behest of his queen, he had been duped by a Gallo-Roman aristocrat.

After Gundobad recovered his strength, and apparently gained the benefit of Visigothic reinforcements,[288] he cavalierly dismissed his tribute to Clovis and attacked his brother Godegisel in Vienne, besieging the city.   Godegisel, running short of provisions, ordered that the commoners be driven out of the city.   Among these people was an engineer who, understandably angered over Godegisel's callous act, told Gundobad of a way into the city via the aqueduct. The engineer led some of Gundobad's men along the aqueduct, through an iron grate and into the city.

Once in the city center, a trumpet was sounded as a signal and Gundobad's forces outside the city walls

---

[287] Kurth, *Saint Clotilda*, 61, 66.

[288] Wolfram, *Germanic Peoples*, 254, elaborated that the presence of the Franks on one side of the Burgundian civil war was enough to attract Alaric II's attention.

crashed the gates and entered the city. According to Gregory, the townspeople were cut to pieces by the two forces. Godegisel hid in an Arian church and was killed with his Arian bishop. Apparently there were still about five thousands Franks who had stayed with Godegisel and Gundobad ordered that they be left alive. His men His men disarmed them and Gundobad exiled them to Toulouse. All of the Burgundians and Gallo-Roman senators who had supported Godegisel were executed.

These events also had wider consequences. The Visigoths received lands from the Burgundians in gratitude for their assistance when Gundobad rewarded Alaric II by ceding Avignon to him in A.D. 501. Gundobad became the sole political figure in the Burgundian kingdom. He had marriage ties to both the Franks and the Ostrogoths of Theodoric, with whom he helped prevent the expansion of Clovis into Provence.

From Clovis's vantage point, his intervention in Burgundian affairs must have made him realize that he had dangerous neighbors to his south-east, both strong in their own right and allied by marriage and circumstance to the Goths. "The Merovingians were seldom astute in their handling of the Burgundians, but they had every excuse to go on trying."[289]

---

[289] Wallace-Hadrill, *The Long-Haired Kings*, 167-69.

Marc A. Comtois

CHAPTER 8
THE REIGN OF GUNDOBAD
(500 A.D. TO 517 A.D.)

The Beginning of his Reign

Under Gundobad, the Burgundian kingdom reached its greatest height. Theodoric and Gundobad had prevented Clovis from conquering Provence and denied him access to the Mediterranean. Yet, the alliances shifted quickly in this era and, after fighting with Clovis in A.D. 500, Gundobad joined him to fight against the Visigoths at Poitiers in A.D. 507. Theodoric did not participate in this war, perhaps because of the complications inherent in siding with one relative against others. On the field of Vouillé, near Poitiers, Alaric fell and Aquitaine was annexed to the dominion of the Franks in A.D. 507. The Franks and the Burgundians had also burned Toulouse, and Gundobad sacked Barcelona. Theodoric had warned Gundobad that an alliance with Clovis would be suicide, but the territorial gains had been apparently too attractive to turn down. In the next few years, Theodoric conducted campaigns in Gaul in which he succeeded in rescuing Arles and in saving Narbonensis for the Visigothic kingdom. He also captured Provence from Burgundy and annexed it to

137

Italy. From A.D. 507-509, the Burgundians lost all of their earlier gains. As the weaker partner in the Frankish-Burgundian alliance, they were the easier mark for Theodoric, who also made devastating forays into their lands.[290]

Despite this territorial setback, Gundobad reigned for sixteen years as sole king of the Burgundians. Under him, the Burgundian kingdom was ruled on the administrative model of Rome even while the military maintained its Germanic characteristics. Most of the Roman-barbarian kingdoms operated with two governmental constants. The first was the executive power in the form of the martial barbarian king and the second was a Roman bureaucracy with a strong emphasis on law.[291] "This gave rise to the union of Roman magisterial structures and Germanic lordship structures. However, the personal element in the exercise of power was derived not only from barbarian tradition but also had roots in the regime of the late-

---

[290] Under Gundobad, Burgundy extended to the northwest as far as Langres, the northern Jura Mountains in the northeast, and the Alps to the east. A portion of the Rhône River and the upper Loire marked its western border and for a brief time, the southern region of Provence was under Burgundian control; see Drew, *Burgundian Code*, 2; Hadrill, *Barbarian West*, 72; *Chronicle of 511* in Murray, *Merovingian Gaul*, 99; Bury, *Roman Empire*, 1:462; and Wolfram, *Germanic Peoples*, 255. Also see Wood, Ian N., "*Gentes*, Kings and Kingdoms—The Emergence of Sates: The Kingdom of the Gibichungs", in *Regna and gentes : the relationship between late antique and early medieval peoples and kingdoms in the transformation of the Roman world*, eds. Hans-Werner Goetz, Jörg Jarnut and Walter Pohl, (Leiden: 2003), for a discussion of how the Burgundian lands didn't in fact become a true kingdom until it fell under Gundobad's control.

[291] Wolfram, *Germanic Peoples*, 116.

antique military emperors."[292] Gundobad sought advice from both Burgundian generals and Gallo-Roman aristocrats and each administrative district included a dualistic judicial system overseen by both a Burgundian *comes* who judged Germans and his Roman counterpart who judged Romans.[293] This system is confirmed in the character of Gundobad's greatest achievement, the *Lex Gundobada*, or Burgundian Code.

The Burgundian Code

One reason for the relative ease with which Romans took to Burgundian rule were the lengths to which the Burgundian rulers went to ensure that Roman citizens were protected. Gregory of Tours said of King Gundobad "He instituted more humane laws for the Burgundians, so they would not oppress the Romans."[294] The recent civil war had shown that Franks and Romans of the senatorial class had been fighting alongside Godegisel, and, Gundobad reasoned that he had to address their concerns. For this reason, he used Roman consults to help him frame his law code.[295]

---

[292] Musset, *Germanic Invasions*, 212.

[293] Ibid., 65.

[294] Gregory of Tours, *History of the Franks*, 148; and Sidonius Apollinaris, *Carmina*. ed. and trans. Christian Luetjohann, *MGH Auctores antiquissimi* 8: 173 ff. 1887, in *Sidonius*, ed. and trans. W.B. Anderson, Loeb Classical Library, 1936. XII: 1-22, in Wolfram, *Germanic Peoples*, 258-59, mentioned that Syagrius, Sidonius' friend, the "Solon of the Burgundians," educated the Burgundians in Latin and Roman laws and society and general. Thus he was able "to implant a 'Latin heart' in the Burgundians," according to Sidonius.

[295] Mathisen, *Roman Aristocrats*, 133; and Dill, *Roman Society*, 65.

"Customary law is a body of moral practices established by the immemorial customs of a people and having a binding moral force rather than the arbitrarily enforced power of statutory law." [296] Statutory law "is a body of specific statures supported by a positive legal authority and guaranteed and enforced by political power."[297] Though customary law may seem less defined and less structured, it is generally more respected because of the moral force behind it and thereby more likely to be obeyed than statutory law. This moral force is buttressed by cultural or traditional expectations and is not as easily ignored as statutory law, which requires some authority to enforce its tenets. The Burgundians brought their customary law with them into the Empire while the Romans who found themselves under the rule of the Burgundians maintained their statutory laws.[298]

From A.D. 474-516, Gundobad undertook the task of codifying both sets of laws. The Burgundian laws are known under many names, such as *Lex Burgundionum, Liber Legum Gundobadi, Lex Gundobada, la Loi Gombette*, and *Gombata* while the laws of the Romans are simply known as the *Lex Romana Burgundionum*. Gundobad's son Sigismund continued

---

[296] Drew, *Burgundian Code*, 3.

[297] Ibid.

[298] Drew, *Burgundian Code*, 3-4; and see Barnwell, *Emperor, Prefects & Kings*, 86, for the observation that the Burgundian law codes were not detailed instructions as much an attempt "to establish general principles" for judges to apply to individual cases. The laws were "didactic and formulaic."

his father's work after A.D. 516 and his brother Godomar also made some contributions during the waning days of the kingdom. The *Lex Gundobada* was a very influential law code and an example of a key transitional stage of law that combined Germanic and Roman laws. The Burgundians had long been exposed to Roman laws and earlier attempts at codifying laws were probably made prior to the *Lex Gundoba*. Allusions to such laws are located throughout the code.[299]

The Burgundians were also assisted more directly in the composition of the laws by Gallo-Roman assistants. These men had both "ideological as well as practical" reasons for offering their assistance. "Romans were used to thinking of their ruler as a source of judgements; it is easy to see why they should have wished barbarian kings to issue written regulations covering disputes between their Roman subjects and their own people, and this helps to account for much of the character of early Visigothic and Burgundian legislation."[300] All of the Burgundian laws set the parameters of personal relationships between individuals; no public law was defined. The *Lex Gundobada* was a trend away from customary law supported by moral ideals toward statutory law based on the political power of a lawgiver, in this case the king.[301]

---

[299] Ibid., 3-8.
[300] David N. Dumville, "Kingship, Genealogies and Regnal Lists," in *Early Medieval Kingship*, ed. Sawyer and Wood, 126-27.
[301] Ibid., 9-10.

The Preface of the code stated that the laws were intended to establish standards for the fair treatment of all classes of subjects. The object throughout is to protect both the rights of the Burgundian settlers and the Romans against further encroachments while promoting peace between the two factions.[302] In order to avoid quarrels, amounts of compensation, called a *wergild*, were set in advance to serve as redemption in lieu of physical acts of vengeance. For example, the Burgundian law said that the life of a freeman was worth 300, 200, or 150 *solidi*. A small pig, still sucking, 3 *solidi*, a small pig already weaned, 1 *solidus*, for a pig two years old, 15 *solidi* plus the payment for the capital and interest. These different amounts were called "compositions."[303] "The payment of this sum did not take the place of public punishment . . . but it cut short all later claims from the parties involved and stopped the exercise of private vengeance."[304]

The class divisions of the Romans and Burgundians in the Burgundian kingdom are not clear, but the *Lex Gundobada* does provide some hints.[305] There were two general divisions of free and unfree with

---

[302] Dill, *Roman Society*, 66-68.

[303] Drew, *Barbarian Code*, 34.

[304] Halphen, "Germanic Society," in Drew, *Barbarian Invasions*, 35.

[305] See Drew, *Burgundian Code*, 19, for the proposition put forth by Professor Summerfield Baldwin that the *wergild* fines given throughout the Code were not meant to be a concrete fine structure. Instead, they were provided as a reference for relative worth, in an attempt to set some value that Romans within Burgundy would understand.

coloni or *originarii* in between. The four classes of free men appear to have been the highest, middle and lowest of free men (who were free from birth) and the freedmen, or slaves who had earned their freedom or had been freed by their masters. The freedmen were the lowest of the free class, but their children were considered to be freemen and a freedman could be considered a freeman following the death of his former master.

The nobles (*optimates*) were the highest class of free men, these were royal servants and officials, but there was no real basis for distinguishing between the middle and lower in the *Lex Gundobada*. Certain characteristics of the laws indicate that the middle class was closer in standing to the upper than the lower class. Intermarriage among the classes of freemen appears to have been common, though the social standing of the offspring of these unions is unknown. Thus, the main distinction between the classes is indicated by the difference in the amount of *wergild* assigned to the life of each man. The *coloni* were lower than freemen, though they were freeborn and recognized as such before the law. They held land, but they couldn't be removed from it nor leave it of their own free will, thus their freedom was limited. Burgundian law didn't recognize social distinctions in the application of penalties, with the exception of differentiating between free and slave. For slaves, the Burgundians were like the Romans whereby they outlined penalties such as lashes of the whip or death whereas they rarely prescribed physical punishment for freemen.[306]

There were only three circumstances in which a freeman or woman was subject to a physical form of punishment. First was a sentence of slavery if a woman was convicted of incest, relations with a slave, or found guilty of complicity if her husband was convicted of stealing horses or cows. Second was the cutting off of the hand if found guilty of forgery or destroying property markers. The third was death in serious cases such as premeditated murder, armed robbery, the venality of judges, or the theft of a slave, horse, ox or cow. "In all other cases, the Burgundian could extricate himself by paying a simple fine the amount of which was fixed in advance (usually 3, 6, or 12 solidi) and added to the composition."[307]

There were protective and restrictive laws that dealt exclusively with women. Daughters weren't allowed admittance to the paternal succession unless there weren't any sons, though they inherited the clothes and ornaments of their mother. However, they made provisions for a woman to inherit property, so long as no sons were alive and she had taken religious vows. In a more somber law, the relatives of a young girl who had been raped were allowed to punish the guilty as they saw fit if the guilty was unable to pay proper compensation, though this was an extreme case. Even if in practice men resorted to violent acts of vengeance to right perceived wrongs done to them, the laws usually

---

[306] Drew, *Burgundian Code*, 41-42, 48.
[307] Halphen, "Germanic Society," in Drew, *Barbarian Invasions*, 38.

placed obstacles to this method and attempted to set up a regular procedure before a court.[308]

The Germanic concept of the family was alive and well in the late fifth and early sixth centuries. The man essentially bought his wife and had to hand to the bride's father an already agreed upon amount, called a *wittimon*. A third of the amount had to be used to buy a trousseau for the bride. Also, after consummation of the marriage, the husband set up a marriage settlement sometimes called the "morning gift," or *morgengabe*.[309] The Burgundians frowned on intermarriage, though they didn't make it illegal, just unprofitable. If, for instance, "a Roman girl, without the consent of knowledge of her parents unites in marriage with a Burgundian, let her know she will have none of the property of her parents."[310]

Burgundian law restricted divorce to cases where the woman had been convicted of adultery or witchcraft or of violating a tomb. If a man's wife committed a crime other than the aforementioned, he had no recourse except to abandon everything to her, which could be an expensive alternative. If he wished to separate from her if she had been found innocent, he risked having to pay her a "composition" equal to the amount of the marriage price (*wittimon*) together with a fine of 12 *solidi* to the treasury. The woman had no

---

[308] Drew, *Burgundian Code*, 32-3; and Halphen, "Germanic Society," in Drew, *Barbarian Invasions*, 34.

[309] Drew, *Burgundian Code*, 35.

[310] Ibid., 31.

recourse, no occasion in which she could be granted divorce. "If she deserted the conjugal hearth, she suffered the penalty of being 'smothered in the mire.'"[311]

Roman influences are seen in an important law that removed "the ancient rule of blame" whereby if an animal owned by a man injured or killed another man or beast of another by accident, the owner of the offending animal was not held liable.[312] The segregation of Roman and Burgundian rights was also safeguarded. Fines were levied to penalize the common practice of Romans petitioning their barbarian overlords to intercede on their behalf in lawsuits between themselves and another Roman, thus reducing the chance that a judge would be swayed by the presence of a barbarian overlord on behalf of one of the plaintiffs.[313]

More Germanic laws can be found under such titles as "Of Those Who Set Traps For Killing Wolves,"[314] "Of Horses Which Have Bones And Sticks Tied To Their Tails,"[315] "Of Hounds, Hunting Dogs, Or Running

---

[311] Halphen, "Germanic Society," in Drew, *Barbarian Invasions,* 36.

[312] Drew, *Burgundian Code*, 35.

[313] Ibid., 39.

[314] Drew, *Burgundian Code*, 53. These traps were of the type called tensuras, or drawn bows. Apparently, people sometimes stumbled into these traps unawares and got hurt or killed. This law defined a specific safety device that was required to be in place. This warning system consisted of two bows, one on either side of the *tensura*, each set to shoot an arrow higher than a man's head so as to send a warning shot that alerted unwary pedestrians of the hidden trap.

[315] Drew, *Burgundian Code*, 69-70. This law stated the offense in the title and described the punishment to be administered based on varying conditions. The *scindola* tied to a horse's tail indicated that someone had

Dogs,"[316] "Of Falcons."[317] These laws provide a more accurate depiction of Burgundian society as it really was than do the more Roman-like, and sophisticated, laws.[318] They reveal that, even at this late date, the Burgundians valued their animals, especially those associated with hunting or war, to a great degree. They also indicate a certain sense of humor, as exhibited by the codification of the penalty whereby one was required to become familiar with a hound's posterior.

Assimilation between Burgundians and Gallo-Romans in the Burgundian kingdom was well underway by the time of Gundobad's reign. Parts of the Burgundian Code made no differentiation between the two, with the same penalties applying to both. Still, total assimilation hadn't occurred, and they were each judged according to different law codes as long as all concerned parties were members of either the Roman or

---

tried to scare the horse to avenge some perceived wrong committed by the horse's master. The hope was that the horse would run around and get hurt or killed. The guilty party was required to pay the owner with a like animal in addition to returning the original to its owner. If the owner didn't want a damaged animal, then two horses of a quality similar to the original were returned to the owner.

[316] Drew, *Burgundian Code*, 47, 84. Here, if anyone was presumed to have stolen a dog "we order that he be compelled to kiss the posterior of that dog publicly in the presence of all the people," or he could pay a fine and a 5 solidi *wergild* to the dog's owner.

[317] Drew, *Burgundian Code*, 84. If anyone was presumed to have stolen another's falcon, he was required to either pay a 6 *solidi wergild* and a 2 *solidi* fine, or "let the falcon eat six ounces of meat from his breast." Some translations had it as eating the meat from the top of his head. Neither would have been pleasant.

[318] Drew, *Burgundian Code*, 70.

Burgundian group. If a mixed conflict arose, then the Burgundian laws held precedent.[319] Full assimilation would only occur when both groups practiced the same version of Christianity.

Christianity in the Burgundian Kingdom

Salvian of Marseille wrote in the 440s that Barbarians are strangers to learning and know nothing unless it is taught to them. Thus, since they were taught heretical, or Arian Christianity, they held that theirs was the true faith and that Catholics were heretical just as the Catholics thought the same of them. This kind of tolerant attitude toward Arian Christians may not have been prevalent, but it may help to explain the tolerance, or at least the lack of antagonism, between the ecclesiastics of each brand of Christianity. According to the historian Salvian, Roman Catholics and barbarian Arians associated rather freely and probably were more unified by the common aspects of Christianity than they were splintered by dogmatic belief in either being the only true form. In Burgundy, the Roman Catholic Church was treated fairly, probably because the royal house had been divided between Arianism and Catholicism.[320]

It seems that, in general, barbarian rulers kept

---

[319] Halphen, "Germanic Society," in Drew, *Barbarian Invasions,* 32.

[320] *Salvian* in Murray, *Merovingian Gaul*, 111-8; Ralph Whitney Mathisen, "Barbarian Bishops and the Churches 'in Barbaricis Gentibus' During Late Antiquity," *Speculum* 72, no.3 (1997): 693-95; see Goffart, "Rome, Constantinople, and the Barbarians", 295-96, for the belief that the Burgundians actually switched from Catholicism to Arianism and back; and Dill, *Roman Society*, 94.

their Arian bishops close at hand and didn't appoint Arian bishops to cities, as was done in the Eastern Empire. They resided near him in his capital and performed services for the king and his retinue, but performed few other ecclesiastical functions. Thus, bishops formed a sort of sacred council and they performed special, mostly diplomatic, missions at the request of the king. Perhaps the barbarian kings were paranoid and sought to keep powerful religious leaders close by to keep an eye on them. History had shown that ecclesiastics often were involved in plots against their overlords.[321]

Gundobad's wife, Caretena, was Catholic, and her "epitaph suggests that she practiced both sexual renunciation and asceticism."[322] According to Fortunatus, "she was...the mother of the poor and the advocate of the guilty" and she also "gave proof on the throne of every virtue, concealing beneath a smiling countenance the fasts and austerities with which she

---

[321] Gregory of Tours, *The History of the Franks,* 137, told the story of how Saint Aprunculus, Bishop of Langres, had become suspicious to the Burgundians because of word of a conspiracy of Catholics in Burgundy with Franks. After the Burgundians put out the order to kill him, Aprunculus "was lowered down from the walls of Dijon" and escaped to Clermont where he was made Bishop; Mathisen in "Barbarian Bishops," 688, wrote of how, when Gundobad captured Vienne, Godegisel fled to an Arian church and was there with an Arian bishop (*cum episcopo arriano*). Mathisen believed that this hinted that the Burgundians had a patriarch, at least in Vienne, whose loyalty to Godegisel was rewarded by death. Or "perhaps this faithful Arian *episcopus* was the chief bishop of Godegisel's sacerdotal college." Finally, Mathisen showed that, with this one exception, there is little evidence of Burgundian Arian bishops.

[322] *Avitus of Vienne*, 213, especially note 2.

subdued her flesh."[323]   Gundobad was friendly with Bishop Avitus of Vienne, who often urged him to convert and may have at least partially succeeded.[324]

Though nominally an Arian and attended to by Arian bishops, Gundobad had a fertile mind and was able to intelligently argue theology with Avitus. He also encouraged debate between Avitus and his Arian bishops. Burgundian Arianism seemed to be based on strict adherence to a literal interpretation of the Latin Bible. This literal familiarity with the Bible was an advantage for Gundobad and his bishops, who proved to be more adept than Avitus in citing specific scriptural passages. Avitus made at least one mistaken identification of a biblical excerpt during a debate with

---

[323] Kurth, *Saint Clotilda*, 20; and Leblant, *Inscriptions Chretiennes de la Gaule*, Vol. I., 70, no. 31, in Kurth, *Saint Clotilda*, 20. Kurth mistakenly thought that this epitaph referred to Clotilda's mother. As has been shown, recent scholarship has attributed this inscription to the wife of Gundobad.

[324] *Avitus of Vienne*, 9; Randers-Pehrson, *Barbarians and Romans*, 266, noted that Avitus' letter to Clovis congratulating him on his baptism must have had to have passed through the hands of Gundobad for approval, "in a way it was addressed more to him than to Clovis." He complimented Clovis for recognizing the true religion, unlike other barbarian rulers, and for breaking with tradition to do so. Thus, any who used tradition as an excuse to hold onto heretical religion no longer had an excuse. "This argument was not lost on Gundobad, who had long wrestled earnestly with the problem and with his conscience."; and James, *The Franks*, 123, who recalled what many historians have forgotten in their discussion of royal conversion; that the process may have had at least three steps. First, the intellectual conversion whereby Christ is accepted; second the public announcement of the acceptance, and third the formal baptism ceremony and acceptance into the Christian community. According to Gregory of Tours, Gundobad reached the first stage but didn't dare take the second for fear of reprisal among the Burgundians.

the Arians, though he may have been citing from memory rather than relying on a direct reference.[325] Despite their theological differences, Gundobad did respect Avitus and asked him to write his 'Against the Eutychian Heresy' after the Trishagion riots in Constantinople in A.D. 511. This illustrated both the scope of his religious inquisitiveness and that he was politically astute enough to want to be on the "right" side of a religious controversy.[326]

Avitus was in line with the orthodox view evolving during his era and was a strong defender of the pope, whose actions he felt only God could ultimately judge. Avitus viewed the controversy surrounding Symmachus and the Laurentian schism as damaging to Catholicism as a whole, and was especially wary of the considerable strength of Arianism among the barbarian kingdoms.[327] In this, as in nearly all other theological writings that passed before the eyes of Gundobad, Avitus wrote on theology "with an eye on the Arianism of the king and his clergy."[328] To these constant entreaties, Gundobad once replied that he couldn't worship the Holy Trinity. Avitus assured Gundobad that he could avert attack, possibly from Clovis and his recently converted Franks, if he simply converted. Gundobad's theological assignment to Avitus prompted Gregory of Tours to believe that Gundobad did

---

[325] *Avitus of Vienne*, 165, which also noted that the Bible used by the Burgundian Arians was written in Latin, not in Ulfilas's original language.

[326] Ibid.,11.

[327] Ibid., 12-13.

[328] Ibid., 11.

eventually convert to Catholic Christianity.[329]

There were instances that seem to indicate that the Burgundians may have encouraged, rather than merely tolerated, Catholicism. Notably, the Catholic bishops of the Burgundian kingdom met at Epaon in A.D. 517, under Avitus, and produced an influential list of canons that served as a basis for laws regarding incest. A pamphlet written by Avitus in A.D. 517, "On Not Assimilating Basilicas of the Heretics," provided additional information regarding the Burgundian Arian church. It was written in response to the fact that Gundobad's son Sigismund had been converted to Catholicism. Avitus had been asked if churches and basilicas of the Arians were to also be converted. Avitus asked if the king had consulted with his Arian bishops and made it clear that the conversion of the king did not mean the conversion of the people. As such, the Arian religion continued to be practiced in Burgundy.[330] Interestingly, Gundobad took much more than a

---

[329] Dill, *Roman Society*, 92; Hen, in his *Culture and Religion*, 13-14, asserted that the barbarians that settled in Gaul left little lasting impression upon the state of Christianity in Gaul. Hen believed that the Arians in Gaul were generally tolerant and even if one doesn't accept this conclusion, Hen pointed out that any persecution was done against Catholicism and not against all Christians; and Gregory of Tours, *The History of the Franks*, 149.

[330] Ian Wood, "Incest, law and the Bible in sixth-century Gaul," *Early Medieval Europe* 7, no.3 (1998): 296. These included prohibitions against marrying your brother's widow, deceased wife's sister, mother-in-law, cousin or child of a cousin, uncle's widow and stepdaughter; *De basilicas haereticorum non recipiendis, Epistulae* 7 (*MGH AA* 6/2:35 – 39) in Mathisen, "Barbarian Bishops," 688; and *Marius Aventicensis, Chronica s.a. 523*, ed. Theodor Mommsen, (*MGH AA* 11:225-39) in Mathisen, "Barbarian Bishops," 688.

philosophical interest in the Catholic church. In A.D. 499, he helped Avitus secure papal recognition making the Bishop of Vienne the primary church authority in Gaul over the bishop of Arles (held by the Goths).[331]

In lands where the ruling class followed their teachings, Arian bishops seemed content and did not actively proselytize among the provincials. "The reason for this was probably the intellectual inferiority of the Arian hierarchy, which was badly equipped for controversy and incapable of contemplating systematic missionary activity."[332] This willingness to allow Catholicism to spread and flourish within the barbarian kingdoms made Arianism less attractive and, ironically, ended a period of dynamic theological thought in Gaul. With no intellectual opponent, Gallo-Roman Orthodox Christian writers lost their rhetorical abilities and became more dogmatic in their theology as they relied on others, especially Augustine, to establish a new "theological uniformity."[333]

The belief that the Burgundians were mostly Arian seems to be an overstated one. Clotilda was a Catholic, as were her sister, and her aunt Caretena. Sidonius indicated that Chilperic I and his wife were friendly with Patiens. The only evidence of an Arian church was during the reign of Gundobad: he killed his

---

[331] Wolfram, *Germanic Peoples*, 258.

[332] Musset, *Germanic Invasions*, 188-89.

[333] *Avitus of Vienne*, 26-27. While the Arian bishops under Gundobad engaged in a theological debate with Avitus, their penchant for being able to memorize and cite specific biblical passages did not necessarily indicate any ability to ponder deeper theological questions.

brother, Godigisil, in one. Yet, again, at this time Clotilda and her sister, and later their cousin Sigismund, were Catholic. With the exception of Gundobad, then, nearly every member of the Burgundian royal family seems to have been a Catholic.[334]

---

[334] Wood, *The Merovingian Kingdoms*, 45, who also theorized that Gundobad may have acquired his Arianism during his younger years in Rome, through his relationship with his uncle Ricimer.

CHAPTER 9
TWILIGHT OF THE BURGUNDIAN KINGDOM
(517 A.D. TO 539 A.D.)

Sigismund and Godomar

Upon Gundobad's death in A.D. 517, his son Sigismund was proclaimed king, while his other son Godomar supported his brother and held court at Geneva.[335] Sigismund had converted to Catholicism, guided by Bishop Avitus of Vienne, probably some time around A.D. 501/502.[336] It has been said that Sigismund was "completely in the hands of Avitus and the Catholic clergy. He looked to the Eastern Emperor as his overlord, and addressed him in almost servile terms."[337] However,

---

[335] Wood, "Kings, Kingdoms and Consent," 22, explained that Sigismund essentially had taken his uncle Godigisil's place as sub-king and Geneva. Upon Gundobad's death, Sigismund was raised to overall king and his brother Godomar filled the subordinate position, and seat, in Geneva.

[336] *Avitus of Vienne*, 18, this dating would place Sigismund's conversion prior to that of Clovis. Shanzer and Wood also noted that "according to Avitus, Sigismund was 'the only one of the kings who was not ashamed to convert'...although strictly speaking he was not the first Catholic Germanic king – that honour must go to Rechiarius, king of the Suevi."

[337] Musset, *Germanic Invasions*, 65; Avitus, *Epp.* 93 and 94 in *Opera*, ed. Piper, 1883, in Bury, *Roman Empire*, 1:463; and see Wolfram, *Germanic Peoples*, 258, who remarked that questions as to whether Sigismund

Sigismund's conversion was probably more a result of a visit to Rome than by any direct influence of Avitus.[338]

The pope or Avitus were not the only Catholics in Sigismund's life. There were many in the Burgundian royalty who were also Catholic, most importantly Sigismund's mother, Caretena. Of course, Sigismund's cousin, Clotilda, was also Catholic, as was her mother and sister. "In fact it is difficult to find named Burgundian women who were Arian."[339] However, Avitus did have a close relationship with Sigismund. On more than one occasion, he wrote to Sigismund to express his disappointment at not having seen him over Easter or when Sigismund had been traveling through Vienne. On other occasions he wrote of his concern for the safety of Sigismund while on a military campaign.[340]

Sigismund had probably been elevated to the position of *rex*, or sub-king, by his father, some time around his conversion.[341] Thus, he was most likely quite an experienced politician by the time his father died and he ascended to the throne. While his father was still alive, he had recognized the precarious position of his kingdom geographically between the Franks and Goths

---

converted because of genuine religious conviction or as a reaction to the conversion of Clovis is unanswerable; and see Wood, *The Merovingian Kingdoms*, 24, for the observation that, though Avitus wasn't necessarily responsible for Sigismund's conversion to Catholicism, "he undoubtedly exercised considerable influence at the start of the new reign."

[338] *Avitus of Vienne*, 9.

[339] Ibid., 19.

[340] *Avitus of Vienne*, 233-241, which encompasses Epistula 45, 76, 77, 79, 91, and 92.

[341] *Avitus of Vienne*, Epistula 8, 220-224, also see Epistula 29, 225-27.

and he sought the aid of the emperor in Byzantium. He wrote to Byzantium to re-assert the status of the Burgundian kingdom as technically a legal territory of the empire, or federated regnum,[342] and to maintain good relations between Constantinople and the Burgundian kingdom.

He reminded the emperor of the role that Burgundy played as a vital part of the empire in Gaul, and, more importantly, lobbied for an imperial position commensurate with one who led such a vital part of the empire.[343] He was rewarded with the title of *patricius* as a result of this correspondence. Upon his assumption of the Burgundian throne, he received the more important title of *magister militum*.[344] These events were noticed by Theodoric, whose own relations with Byzantium had crumbled. He attempted to cut off diplomatic traffic between the two, most of which were letters written by Avitus of Vienne, by not allowing Sigismund's messengers to travel through Italy to Constantinople.[345]

Sigismund had a few important accomplishments. He built a monastery at Saint-Maurice d'Agaune in A.D. 515 and the monks supported him. He added to the *Lex Gundobad*. Lyons, and possibly Vienne, had schools of rhetoric and archeologists have traced Latin inscriptions to this period. It was he who, in A.D. 517, had called for the

---

[342] Wolfram, *Germanic Peoples*, 256.

[343] *Avitus of Vienne*, Epistula 46a and 47, 138-39; and Wolfram, *Germanic Peoples*, 256.

[344] Ibid., Epistula 93, 146-48.

[345] Avitus, *Epp.* 94, in *Opera*, (1883), in Bury, *Roman Empire*, 1:463.

royal synod at Epaon and who also held several provincial synods during his reign.[346]

Unfortunately, the murderous palace scandal resulted in a "no-confidence" vote by the Catholic bishops and contributed greatly to erosion of ecclesiastical support for Sigismund. Though a resolution was made, Sigismund would never recapture the same standing among the ecclesiastics that he had once held.[347] Additionally, the revenue stream, increasingly reliant upon the a shrinking pool of Gallo-Roman landholders who saw no such taxation requirements put upon their exempted Burgundian neighbors, may have been drying up.[348] Thus, while the money supply shrank, the resentment among those contributing to it grew.

Sigismund also had problems within his immediate family. His first wife, the daughter of the Ostrogothic King Theodoric, had died giving birth to his eldest son Sigeric. According to Gregory of Tours' account, Sigismund's second wife disliked Sigeric and

---

[346] Wolfram, *Germanic Peoples*, 258; and *Avitus of Vienne*, 22-23.

[347] See Wood, *Law and the Bible*, 299-300, for the explanation that the Catholic bishops were disappointed by Sigismund's actions in a case involving his royal treasurer Stephanus in an incestuous relationship with a woman named Palladia; and *Avitus of Vienne*, 23-24. For more on the palace scandal, see page 118, below.

[348] Musset, *Germanic Invasions*, 212-13, "Everywhere, in fact, the fundamental resources of the state continued to be provided by the Roman taxation system, the burden of which rested on the Roman inhabitants, through the medium of a government land survey whose registers continued to be kept more or less up to date; the general exemption from taxes which the barbarian estates enjoyed must have diminished the yield as well as increased the burden."

conspired to make Sigismund suspicious of Sigeric's motives towards his father. She convinced him that Sigeric was conspiring with his grandfather Theodoric to seize Burgundy from Sigismund. Her conniving was successful and Sigismund made plans to have Sigeric murdered. He got his son drunk until he passed out and then had two retainers strangle him. He immediately regretted his act as he "threw himself on the dead body and wept most bitterly."[349] Burgundian outrage at this vicious murder combined with the recent loss of ecclesiastical support proved to be Sigismund's undoing. He might have survived, despite this internal unrest, had not external factors also contributed to his downfall.

According to Gregory, Clotilda asked her sons to avenge her father's death on the sons of Gundobad. In 523, Clovis's son Clodomir, marched against the Burgundians and defeated them. Despite any technical alliance with Byzantium, the reality was that the Burgundians simply didn't have the military might to ward off their enemies. Memories of Roman titles may have been pleasant, but they were of no practical help.[350]

Godomar escaped, but while Sigismund and his

---

[349] Gregory of Tours, *The History of the Franks*, 165-66; also see *Marius of Avenches* in Murray, *Merovingian Gaul*, 103, which mentioned that "Segeric, the son of Sigismund, was unjustly killed by order of his father."; and Kurth, *Saint Clotilda*, 77, noted that, unfortunately, though Sigismund was generous, intelligent and pious, he was also weak-minded and prone to "changeable humour," and after the death of Avitus, his second wife gained the most influence upon him.

[350] Wolfram, *Germanic Peoples*, 256.

family tried to seek refuge in the monastery of Agaune, Clodomir captured and held them hostage. According to another source, some Burgundians had given Sigismund to the Franks. This may be more accurate. Many Burgundians, outraged at his past actions, willingly turned Sigismund over. Meanwhile, Godomar reassembled his forces and won back at least a portion of the kingdom. Clodomir prepared to attack Godomar and decided to kill Sigismund, apparently to rid himself of the distraction. Despite the pleas of Avitus, he ordered Sigismund and his entire family thrown down a well.[351]

Marius of Avenches wrote that, in A.D. 524, "Godomar, the brother of Sigismund, was appointed king of the Burgundians."[352] Clodomir then summoned his brother Theuderic, who agreed to march in support of Clodomir against Godomar. They marched to Vezeronce and fought Godomar, who fled with his army. Clodomir followed in close pursuit, but raced too far in front of his troops. Godomar's men killed him and put his head on a stake as a grisly trophy. Clodomir's Franks saw this, rallied and harried Godomar out of his lands again. Godomar had not been fighting only the Franks.

---

[351] Gregory of Tours, *The History of the Franks*, 166-67; and *Marius of Avenches* in Murray, *Merovingian Gaul*, 103, who wrote that Sigismund was led into Francia, dressed as a monk and then "thrown into a well with his wife and children."

[352] *Marius of Avenches* in Murray, *Merovingian Gaul*, 103; and *Avitus of Vienne*, 22, Godomar may have been son to Gundobad by a second wife and considerably younger than his brother. He may also have been converted to Catholicism at the same time as his brother.

Sigismund's murder of Sigeric had enraged the child's grandfather, Theodoric, who invaded southern Burgundy at the same time, with much Burgundian support. It was at this time that Theodoric made his famous agreement with the sons of Clovis whereby he acquired half of the lands of Burgundy for the loss of no blood and only a little treasure.[353]

As mentioned, Gregory placed the revenge of Clotilda at the center of the Frankish desire to conquer Burgundy.[354] Yet, as has already been discussed, Clotilda

---

[353] "In this year, he fought against Chlodomer, king of the Franks, at Vezeronce and there Chlodomer was killed" in *Marius of Avenches* in Murray, *Merovingian Gaul*, 103; Gregory of Tours, *The History of the Franks*, 167; Procopious of Caesarea, *De Bello Gothico*, Bonn ed. in Dill, *Roman Society*, 158; Procopius, *History of the Wars, Books V and VI*, trans. by H.B. Dewing in *Procopius*. Loeb Classical Library (Cambridge, Mass.: Harvard University Press, 1953), 3:125, 127.

[354] Wolfram, *Germanic Peoples*, 256, noted both the Franks and Theodoric's Goths invaded Burgundy, claiming revenge as a reason "that may well have been intended merely to veil hard power politics."; also see Kurth, *Saint Clotilda*, 139-140, who offered a viable counterargument to Gregory's account. "If Clotilda was so eager for vengeance why did she not urge the duty on her husband Clovis, and why did she wait for the death of [Gundobad] in order to vent her wrath upon the innocent son of the latter?" He supported his belief with the fact that when Clovis had Gundobad within his power at Vienne, he left the field. Even when Gundobad failed to send tribute the next year, Clovis did not go to war with him. Instead, he made an alliance, "and all this under the very eyes of Clotilda just at the time of his own conversion to Christianity, when we may presume that his wife's influences was most potent with him." Given this, it seemed Clotilda, if she had wrongs to avenge, must have forgotten them until after both Clovis, her "natural avenger" and Gundobad were dead. "[I]t was only after both offender and offended had been in their graves the one during nine and the other during twelve years, and when there was nobody to punish, that we are asked to believe that this pious widow, living in retirement and devoting herself to good works, separated from her sons

may have had nothing to avenge. She probably arranged the original alliance between Clovis and Gundobad around A.D. 507. This act of diplomacy would be difficult to accept of a woman with vitriolic hatred for her uncle.[355] Further, if Clotilda had "waited from the A.D. 490s until A.D. 523 the feud cannot have been uppermost in her mind."[356]

Some believed that the story was invented by popular imagination in an attempt to explain the reason that led two closely allied families to go to war. Accordingly, a connection was made by portraying the story of Gundobad's murder of Chilperic and his wife first to justify the nearly identical form of Clotilda's supposed revenge. Because Clodomir killed Sigismund

---

and peacefully awaiting death, suddenly bethought herself to crown a life filled with good works by initiating a fratricidal war in which her own flesh and blood were to perish."; for a retort, see Wemple, *Women in Frankish Society*, 60, which made the interesting argument that since "Loyalty to the uterine line was inculcated in aristocratic males in their early childhood... we should not be surprised to learn that Clotild[a] asked her sons, not her husband, to avenge the murder of her parents."; Also see *Avitus of Vienne*, 210, in which it was the duality between this and the supposed murder of Chilperic and his wife was noted. The authors also assigned the same penchant for fratricide and patricide among "many of the opponents of Clovis and his sons, including the Thuringians, Ostrogoths, Visigoths and Burgundians." Given this, "the accusation may, therefore, have been an aspect of Merovingian political propaganda." To this I might add that it is a common tactic in politics to accuse your opponent of those things that you have or would do. Could Gregory have ascribed so many instances of inter-family murder in an attempt to portray such acts as commonplace, thus diminishing the horrendousness of the crime often committed by the ancestors of his own Merovingian patrons?

[355] Godefroid Kurth, "St. Clotilda," in *Catholic Encyclopedia*, 1908 ed.
[356] Wood, *The Merovingian Kingdoms*, 43.

and his wife, the legend grew that Chilperic's wife, (Clotilda's mother) was killed with him and both thrown in a well. Because Clodomir also killed Sigismund's two remaining sons, then Gundobad was said to have killed Chilperic's two sons (though these may have never actually existed).[357]

"We can thus safely conclude that the true Gundobad was not the sanguinary tyrant of later tradition, nor was Clotilda the bearer of tragedy and doom to the Burgundian house as she appears in the story."[358]   A parallel can be drawn in the similarity

---

[357] Bury, *Invasion of Europe*, 235-8; and Wood, *The Merovingian Kingdoms*, 43, "There is also a curious parallel between the manner of [Chilperic II's] death, supposedly by drowning in a well, and the similar disposal of Sigismund's body after his defeat and capture in 524. It seems that Gregory's account of the murder of Chilperic and the subsequent bloodfeud reflected later assumptions, rather than historical reality. The marriage of [Clotilda], therefore, may not have had the ominous implications which the bishop of Tours attributed it."; and Kurth, *Saint Clotilda*, 140-41, explained this legend grew up because of "the universal tendency of the popular mind to explain great misfortunes as being the expiation of great crimes. When Sigismund, king of Burgundy, was killed with his wife and children by his cousin Clodomir, it was supposed that he must have perished in expiation of some similar crime which one of his ancestors had perpetrated against some member of Clodomir's family. And hence it was easy to assume that [Gundobad] had inflicted on Chilperic, the grandfather of Clodomir, the same treatment as, at a later date, Clodomir had inflicted on his son."

[358] Bury, *Invasion of Europe*, 238; and Kurth, *Saint Clotilda*, 78-9, for the observation that for "the pretext on which the sons of Clovis took up arms against their unhappy cousin we have no information, nor indeed is the question of much historic importance. The war may have been caused simply by that insatiable love of fighting and of glory which lies at the root of uncivilised [sic] nature, or again by that desperate avarice which gave men no rest so long as there remained anything to covet or to conquer."

between Gregory's account of Clovis's battlefield conversion and that of Constantine roughly two hundred years earlier. Gregory was not above using one event as a template for another if he deemed it convenient or necessary. After all, Gregory and Fredegarius were Merovingian chroniclers and probably desired to show their patrons in the best light, often at the expense of historical truth.

Regardless of the version of the tale of the death of Gundobad's heir, Godomar and his men did kill Clodomir in the battle of Vezeronce, in A.D. 524. Gregory recounted that Clotilda took Clodomir's three sons into her care, but she could not save them from their own uncles. Childebert and Lothar had divided between them the inheritance of their elder brother. They did not wish the children to live and one day properly claim their inheritance. By means of a ruse, they spirited the children from their mother and slew the two eldest. With help from his grandmother, the third, and youngest, escaped and entered a cloister. Distraught, Clotilda divested herself of her wealth by donating it to churches and monasteries and left Paris for Tours where she could be close to the tomb of her patron, Saint Martin. She spent the remainder of her life in prayer and doing good works. Meanwhile, Godomar returned yet again and retook Burgundy, if only temporarily.[359]

---

[359] Gregory of Tours, *The History of the Franks*, 180-2; and Kurth, "St. Clotilda."; and Scherman, *Birth of France*, 142; and Gregory's one line afterthought in *The History of the Franks*, 167, that "Godomar won back his

After Theodoric died in A.D. 526, and after a conquest in Spain to return their sister, Clotilda II, home, Lothar and Childebert decided to attack Burgundy again. Theuderic refused to join them, but his men, who desired loot, threatened to desert if he did not take part. He promised them all of the Burgundian loot they could carry as long as they did not to join his brothers. His men agreed and they marched into Clermont and brought as much as they could, both goods and people, away from the city. While Theuderic and his men were looting and capturing slaves, Lothar and Childebert besieged Autun in A.D. 534 and forced Godomar to flee Burgundy a final time.[360]

Godomar may have also overestimated his position. In A.D. 530, he had made a treaty with Amalasuintha, the Ostrogothic queen and regent. It called for mutual assistance between the two kingdoms. This had provided Godomar with some additional military might, so he thought, in exchange for the cessation of the territory north of the Durance to the young Ostrogothic king. However, when attacked by the Franks again in A.D. 532, the Ostrogothic army only fought to reestablish its former borders. Finally, in A.D.

---

kingdom a third time."
[360] Gregory of Tours, *The History of the Franks*, 170-71; Procopius, *History of the Wars*, 3:133, 135, who recounted that the Franks captured Godomar and kept him in a fortress while they subjugated his people and forced them to fight with the Franks in battle. The "whole land which the Burgundians had previously inhabited they made subject and tributary to themselves."; and *Marius of Avenches* in Murray, *Merovingian Gaul*, 103, wrote that the Franks took Burgundy, divided it and caused King Godomar to flee.

534, the Ostrogothic army offered no aid and left Godomar to his fate.[361] He disappeared forever and so did Burgundian rule in Burgundy. The aristocracy continued to operate and at least some members, or descendents, of the former royal family survived until 613.[362] However, the last significant act by a group of Burgundians would be that of a band of warriors, who, by the direction of the new ruler, had a final curtain call on the stage of history.

Italian Coda

In A.D. 539, during the early years of Emperor Justinian's invasion of Italy, the newly-crowned Ostrogoth king Vittigis sought to bolster his defense against the Imperial forces led by Belisarius. He requested the assistance of Theudibert (A.D. 533-48), the Frankish king of Burgundy, who agreed to send aid and did so in the form of 10,000 Burgundians. This enabled Theudibert to claim that he was doing nothing to hurt the Emperor's cause as the Burgundians acted on their own accord and not by his command. The Burgundians assisted the Goths in the siege of the weakly garrisoned city of Milan.[363] Attempts to relieve the city were mishandled, and while reinforcements dallied, the siege was having its desired affect. Milan was on the verge of famine.

---

[361] Wolfram, *Germanic Peoples*, 257.

[362] Musset, *Germanic Invasions*, 148.

[363] Procopius, *History of the Wars*, 3:395, 397; and Collins, *Early Medieval Europe*, 129-33.

The Burgundians and Goths sent envoys to Mundilas, the Milan garrison commander, and asked him to surrender the city. Mundilas attempted to extract from the barbarians a promise to cause no harm to the inhabitants of the city. However, "the enemy, though ready to give pledges to Mundilas and the soldiers, were moved by furious passion against the Ligurians and were evidently going to destroy all."[364] Despite the entreaties of Mundilas, all of his soldiers chose surrender over honorable death. The barbarians left the soldiers alone, "but the city they razed to the ground, killing all the males of every age to the number of not less than three hundred thousand."[365] The Burgundians received the women as slaves as repayment for their alliance, and seemed to disappear. This was the final act of a distinctly Burgundian army. After this brief episode, they simply became another group assimilated into Merovingian France and vanished into the mist.

---

[364] Procopius, *History of the Wars*, 55, noted under A.D. 538 that "Milan was stormed by the [Ostro]Goths and Burgundians, and there senators and priests along with other people were killed even in the holy places, so that the altars were stained with their blood."; and *Marius of Avenches* in Murray, *Merovingian Gaul*, 104.

[365] Procopius, *History of the Wars*, 57.

Marc A. Comtois

EPILOGUE

After the murders of her grandsons, Queen Clotilda lived a life of chastity and charity in Tours.[366] She made many private donations. In Clermont, she gave a priest, named Anastasius, a gift of land and commensurate title. The Bishop of Clermont, Cautinus, sought to keep the lands for himself by dint of his authority, but Anastasius maintained his rights to the land, even after being tortured. Anastasius eventually escaped and complained to King Lothar, who upheld the legitimacy of Clotilda's gift.[367] "Thus the most ancient Merovingian deed of gift of which we have authentic knowledge, issued from the hand of our Saint, and testifies to an act of generosity performed by her."[368]

---

[366] See *Sainted Women of the Dark Ages*, ed. and trans. JoAnn McNamara and John E. Halborg with E. Gordon Whatley (Durham, N.C.: Duke University Press, 1992), 40, where it is hypothesized that Clotilda went to Tours in the relatively newly acquired Aquitaine, where Clovis was commissioned as patrician of Rome, as "part of an ongoing Frankish policy of reaching a solid settlement with the old Gallo-Roman population."

[367] Gregory of Tours, *Historia Francorum*, 4.12, in Kurth, *Saint Clotilda*, 108; and see *Sainted Women of the Dark Ages*, 49, n.42, where it is noted that female saints "regularly diminished the gains of their warrior relatives by almsgiving." This "suggests that they were playing a sort of structural role in the circulation of wealth, possibly as representatives of the more merciful or 'womanly' side of monarchy."

[368] Kurth, *Saint Clotilda*, 108.

She also funded the building of many churches and monasteries and gave lands to support them. Among these was the Notre-Dame-des-Andelys, located along the Seine near Rouen, around whose founding and construction a story was told concerning Clotilda. [369]

According to the story, the men working on the church requested of Clotilda that wine be provided to slake their thirst during the hot summer days. While she considered the request, a spring of fresh water was discovered nearby. In a dream, Clotilda was told that if the workers were to request wine again, that she should send a servant to take them some water from this newfound spring. When the request was made, and the water delivered, the workers discovered that the water had turned to wine. They went to the queen and gave thanks. The queen gave credit to God for the miracle and asked none to reveal the miracle. The situation continued throughout the construction of the monastery, but only occurred for the workmen working on the structure. All others who drank the water tasted water. When the monastery was completed, the miracle ended and the spring returned to its natural state for one and all. [370]

Clotilda did not totally remove herself from the lives of her sons, and perhaps her most famous miracle was associated with her concern for their welfare. According to Gregory, her son Childebert and step-grandson Theudebert were at war with her son Lothar,

---

[369] Ibid., 105.

[370] *Vita Sanctae Chrotildis*, c. XII, in Kurth, *Saint Clotilda*, 105-6.

who had the weakest army of the three. He retreated to a forest near Caudebec in Normandy and entrenched himself and prayed for his safety. His mother also prayed for the intercession of St. Martin in hopes of averting another family tragedy. When Childebert came near Lothar's position, a thunderstorm occurred, lightning flashed, the wind howled, and hailstones fell. Soldiers covered themselves with their shields and horses ran away. Meanwhile, those in Lothar's camp heard nothing, all was quiet and no storm raged. Unnerved, Childebert and Theodebert begged for God's mercy and retreated. Peace was made with Lothar and each returned to their own lands. Her prayers were said to have inspired St. Martin's miracle.[371]

Miracles aside, she also seems to have rewarded some Burgundian religious men who had accompanied her to Clovis' kingdom. In the years 520 and 521, she appointed three elderly men to be Bishops of Tours. Clotilda herself died in Tours in 545 A.D. and was carried to Paris and buried by her sons Childebert and Lothar in Saint Peter's church next to her husband Clovis.[372]

---

[371] Gregory of Tours, *The History of the Franks*, 185-86; and Kurth, *Saint Clotilda*, 97-98.

[372] Gregory of Tours, *The History of the Franks*, 598, 197. He wrote that Theodorus and Proculus, the tenth Bishops of Tours, had come with Clotilda from Burgundy as consecrated Bishops but "had been expelled from their cities because they had incurred hostility there." She appointed them jointly in early A.D. 520 when they were old men. They led Tours for two years before dying and being buried there. Dinifius, who had also come from Burgundy, succeeded to the Bishop's office at the behest of Clotilda in A.D. 521. She gave him property from the royal domain to do with as he wished. He gave most of it to his own cathedral and left the rest for

"Neither the royal status of her sons nor her worldly goods nor earthly ambition could bring her to disrepute. In all humility she moved forward to heavenly grace."[373] Through her piety, Clotilda served as a light in the darkness for the barbarians heirs to Rome. The greatest Queen of the Franks was a Burgundian and, through her, the first real king of the Franks was Christianized and secured the faith in Europe.[374]

"deserving people." He was only Bishop for ten months.

[373] Gregory of Tours, *The History of the Franks*, 182.

[374] Schulenburg, *Forgetful of Their Sex*, 180, argues Clotilda became the prototype for later Catholic queens; and Scherman, *The Birth of France*, 142-43, wrote that "[Clotilda's] selfless dedication is the obverse side of the Merovingian nature...the pure and literal application of the teaching of the primitive Church. People like Clotild[a]...add a dimension of light, like the sun shining in back of a cloud, to the dismal and stormy climate of post-imperial Europe." Of course, it must be remembered that Clotilda was, in fact, a Burgundian.

REFERENCE MATERIAL

Marc A. Comtois

Timeline of Burgundian History

c.100 - Burgundians, originating in Scandinavia, migrated east toward the Vistula.

c.166 - Marcommanic Wars began and lasted until A.D. 180.

c.250 - Burgundians began westward movement and raided Roman territory.

c.274 - Burgundians possibly among those who raided Gaul and sacked Trier.

277 - Probus embarked on campaign in Gaul against Germans, probably including Burgundians.

359 - Burgundian settlements reached east bank of Rhine no later than this date.

369 - Valentinian I used Burgundians against Alamanni.

406 - Rhine froze and Burgundians followed Vandals and Alans across river.

407 - Burgundians held region along West bank of Rhine, near Koblenz.

409 - By this time, Burgundians had fought and pushed Alamanni out of region and occupied territory on both sides of Rhine. They came in contact with Constantine III.

411 - Burgundians supported Jovinus as Emperor.

413 - Honorius accepted Burgundians as *foederati* and first Burgundian kingdom established near Koblenz.

435 - Burgundians embarked on many raids and plots to extend territory at expense, and against the wishes, of Rome. Believed to have been converted to Arian Christianity by this time.

436 - Aëtius punished Burgundians for their attempts at expansion by first attacking them with his own forces, then with the Huns. This is the inspiration of the *Nibelungenlied*. Several thousand Burgundians killed, including King Gundahar.

443 - Remaining Burgundians resettled by Aëtius in region around Geneva (Sapaudia).

451 - Battle of Chalons. Burgundians fought on both sides, with Gundioc leading the Burgundians opposed to Attila.

455 - Burgundians supported Avitus as Emperor.

456 - Burgundian kings Gundioc and Chilperic I accompanied Theoderic II in campaign against Sueves in Spain.

457 - Burgundians seized large portions of Lugdunensis I and Viennensis, but withdrew in face of Marjorian.

461 - After Marjorian's death, Burgundian rulers accepted imperial military titles and named as patricians.

463 - Burgundians took Die.

c.470 - Gundobad traveled to Rome and entered service of his uncle Ricimer.

472 - Olybrius established as Roman emperor, raised Gundobad to patrician upon death of Ricimer.

473 - Glycerius established as Roman emperor by Gundobad, but not supported by Emperor Leo in Constantinople. Julius Nepos sent West to assume throne.

474 - Gundioc died. Kingdom is split between sons Chilperic, Gundobad, Godigisel and Gundomar. Gundobad left Rome for Burgundy to assume throne. Clotilda, daughter of Chilperic I, was born, probably in Lyons. By this time, Vaison and Lyons under Burgundian control, though the latter may have been so as early as A.D. 461.

485 - By this time Langres was under Burgundian control. After Chilperic died of either natural causes, or with fraternal assistance, Gundobad and Godegisel shared rule of Burgundian kingdom with Gundobad as the primary king.

490 - Burgundians under Gundobad supported Odovacer against Theodoric, either directly or indirectly. Gundobad raided northern Italy.

493 - Clovis and Clotilda formally betrothed in Chalon.

494 - Epiphanius, ambassador of Theodoric, received by Gundobad in Lyons. Sigismund, son of Gundobad, and a daughter of Theodoric betrothed to strengthen political alliance.

500 - By this time, Burgundians dominated most of eastern Gaul from southern limits of Champagne to the Alps. Civil war began in Burgundy as Franks supported Godegisel and join in an attempt to defeat Gundobad. Result of war was the death of Godegisel and Gundobad became sole King of the Burgundians.

507 - Gundobad and Clovis fought against Alaric and the Visigoths in Poitiers, and Gundobad sacked Barcelona.

511 - Clovis, King of the Franks, died. Clotilda may have had a hand in partitioning of the Frank kingdom amongst her sons and stepson. Clotilda resided in Paris and fretted over her progeny.

516 - Beginning in A.D. 474, *Lex Gundobada* compiled and published by this time.

517 - Gundobad died, Sigismund assumed Burgundian throne with his brother Godomar taking the heir's seat in Geneva. Sigismund, already Catholic, built a monastery at Saint-Maurice d'Agaune around this time.

c.520 - Three successive Burgundians named Bishop of Tours by Queen Clotilda.

c.522 - Sigismund killed Segeric, his son by Theodoric's daughter. Theodoric was not pleased.

523 - Clodomir, son of Clovis, invaded Burgundian kingdom. He captured and killed Sigismund and his family, probably with the help of some Burgundians, by throwing them down a well. Theodoric also involved in attacks on Burgundians.

524 - Godomar appointed king of the Burgundians and faced Franks and Theodoric. Fought Clodomir's Franks and killed Clodomir at Vezeronce, but driven out of his lands by Clodomir's men. Franks and Theodoric split captured portions of Burgundian Kingdom. Clotilda withdrew to Tours after two of Clodomir's sons, who had been left in her care, are murdered by their uncles Lothar and Childebert.

534 - Lothar and Childebert besieged Autun and forced Godomar to flee. They are said to have destroyed the remnants of the Burgundian ruling family. Burgundian lands integrated into Merovingian dynasty.

539 - Burgundian warriors took part in Goth siege of Milan.

545 - Clotilda, Burgundian princess and Queen of the Franks, died.

613 - Some members of the former Burgundian royal family said to have survived at least until this time.

Marc A. Comtois

List of Works Cited

Primary Sources

Avitus, *Epistulae,* 93 and 94. Edited by R. Peiper, *Alcimi Ecdicii Aviti Viennensis episcopi. Opera quae supersunt, Monumenta Germaniae historica, Auctores antiquissimi 6.2* (Berlin, 1883). In J.B. Bury, *History of the Later Roman Empire: From the Death of Theodosius I. to the Death of Justinian,* 1:463. New York: Dover Publications, Inc., 1958.

_____. *Avitus of Vienne: Letters and Selected Prose.* Translated with an Introduction by Danuta Shanzer and Ian Wood. *Translated Texts for Historians*, Vol. 38. Liverpool: Liverpool University Press, 2002.

The Burgundian Code. Translated by Katherine Fischer Drew with a Foreword by Edward Peters. 4th ed. Philadelphia: University of Pennsylvania Press, 1992.

Cassius Dio, 56.18.2. In Whittaker, C.R. *Frontiers of the Roman Empire: A Social and Economic Study*, 131. Baltimore: The Johns Hopkins University Press, 1994.

Chronica Gallica A. CCCCLII. Edited by Th. Mommsen, *Chronica Minor I, Monumenta Germaniae historica, Auctores antiquissimi 9* (Berlin: 1892), 646-662. Translated by A.C. Murray. In *From Roman to Merovingian Gaul: A Reader,* ed. and trans. Alexander Callander Murray, 76-85. Orchard Park, NY: Broadview Press, 2000.

Chronica Gallica, DXI. Edited by Th. Mommsen *Chronica Minor I, Monumenta Germaniae historica, Auctores antiquissimi 9* (Berlin: 1892), 664-666. Translated by A.C. Murray. In *From Roman to Merovingian Gaul: A Reader,* ed. and trans. Alexander Callander Murray, 98-100. Orchard Park, NY: Broadview Press, 2000.

Chronica a. CCCCLV-DLXXXI. Edited by Th. Mommsen, *Chronica Minora 2, Monumenta Germaniae historica, Auctores antiquissimi 11* (Berlin: 1894), 225-39. Translated by A.C. Murray. In *From Roman to Merovingian Gaul: A Reader,* ed. and trans. Alexander Callander Murray, 100-108. Orchard Park, NY: Broadview Press, 2000.

The Chronicle of Hydatius and the Consularia Constantinopolitana. Edited and Translated by Richard W. Burgess (Oxford, 1993). Translated by A.C. Murray. In *From Roman to Merovingian Gaul: A Reader,* ed. and trans. by Alexander Callander Murray, 85-98. Orchard Park, NY: Broadview Press, 2000.

De basilicas haereticorum non recipiendis, Epistulae 7, Monumenta Germaniae historica, Auctores antiquissimi 6/2:35 – 39. In Ralph Whitney Mathisen, *Roman Aristocrats in Barbarian Gaul: Strategies for Survival in an Age of Transition,* 688. Austin: University of Texas Press, 1993.

The Elder Edda of Saemund Sigfusson. Translated by Benjamin Thorpe and *The Younger Edda of Snorre Sturleson.* Translated by I.A. Blackwell. Edited by Rasmus B. Anderson. London: Norrœna Society, 1907.

Ennodius, *Opera.* Edited by Hartel, *Hist. Misc.* 15.16 (1882), 276, 369. In J.B Bury, *History of the Later Roman Empire: From the Death of Theodosius I. to the Death of Justinian,* 1:424-5, 427. New York: Dover Publications, Inc., 1958.

The Fourth Book of the Chronicle of Fredegar with its Continuations. Translated with Introduction by J.M. Wallace-Hadrill. London: Thomas Nelson and Sons Ltd., 1960.

Fredegarius. *Scholasticus, Chronicarum libri 2.46*. Edited by B. Krusch, *Monumenta Germaniae historica, Scriptores rerum merovingicarum* 2 (Berlin, 1888), 68. In Walter Goffart, *Barbarians and Romans, A.D. 418-584: The Techniques of Accommodation*, 107. Princeton: Princeton University Press, 1980.

_____. *Historia Francorum Epitomata*. Edited by Migne, lxxi. In Samuel Dill, *Roman Society in Gaul in the Merovingian Age*, 83-4. London: George Allen & Unwin Ltd., 1926.

Gregory of Tours. *The History of the Franks*. Translated with an Introduction by Lewis Thorpe. London: Penguin Books, 1974.

Hilarius, Bishop of Rome, *Epistulae* "Qualiter contra sedis," *Monumenta Germaniae historica, Epistulae* 3.28-29. In Ralph Whitney Mathisen, *Roman Aristocrats in Barbarian Gaul: Strategies for Survival in an Age of Transition,* 73. Austin: University of Texas Press, 1993.

Jordanes, *The Origins and Deeds of the Goths*. Translated by Charles C. Mierow. [book on-line]. Princeton, NJ: Princeton University Press, 1915. Available from <www.northvegr.org/lore/pdf/jordanes.pdf>. Accessed 19 March 2004.

La Chronique de Marius d'Avenches (455-581), Edited and Translated by Justin Favrod, 2nd ed. (Lausannne, 1993). Translated by A.C. Murray. In *From Roman to Merovingian Gaul: A Reader,* ed. and trans. by Alexander Callander Murray, 100-108. Orchard Park, NY: Broadview Press, 2000.

Marcellinus , Ammianus. *The Surviving Books of the History*. Translated by John C. Rolfe. 3 vols. *Ammianus Marcellinus*. Loeb Classical Series. Cambridge, Mass.:

Harvard University Press, 1939.

Marius Aventicensis, *Chronica s.a. 523*. Edited by Theodor Mommsen, *Monumenta Germaniae historica, Auctores antiquissimi* 11:225-39 (Berlin: 1894). In Ralph Whitney Mathisen, "Barbarian Bishops and the Churches 'in Barbaricis Gentibus' During Late Antiquity," *Speculum* 72, no.3 (1997): 688.

Monumenta Germaniae historica, Rerum merovingicarum Ii, iii, 18-19. Edited by Krusch, 89 ff. (1888). In Samuel Dill, *Roman Society in Gaul in the Merovingian Age*, 83-4. London: George Allen & Unwin Ltd., 1926.

Orosius, Paulus. *Historiae adv. Paganos*. Edited by Zangemeister (1889). In J.B Bury, *History of the Later Roman Empire: From the Death of Theodosius I. to the Death of Justinian,* 1:189. New York: Dover Publications, Inc., 1958.

_____. *The Seven Books of History Against the Pagans*. Translated by Roy J. Deferrari. Vol. 50. *The Fathers of the Church*. Washington, D.C.: Catholic University of America Press, 1964.

Pliny. *Natural History*. Vol. 2. Translated by H. Rackham. Loeb Classical Series. Cambridge, Mass.: Harvard University Press, 1942.

Procopious of Caesarea, *De Bello Gothico*, Bonn ed. In Samuel Dill, *Roman Society in Gaul in the Merovingian Age*, 158. London: George Allen & Unwin Ltd., 1926.

_____. *History of the Wars, Books V and VI* . Translated by H.B. Dewing. Vol. 3, *Procopius*. Loeb Classical Series. Cambridge, Mass.: Harvard University Press, 1953.

_____. *History of the Wars, Books VI (continued) and VII*. Translated by H.B. Dewing. Vol. 4, *Procopius*. Loeb Classical Series. Cambridge, Mass.: Harvard University Press, 1954.

The Prose Edda of Snorri Sturluson: Tales from Norse Mythology. Introduction by Sigurdur Nordal. Translated by Jean I. Young. Berkeley: University of California Press, 1966.

Prosperi Tironis epitoma chronicon. Edited by Th. Mommsen, *Chronica Minora I, Monumenta Germaniae historica, Auctores antiquissimi 9* (1892), 385-485. Translated by A.C. Murray. In *From Roman to Merovingian Gaul: A Reader,* ed. and trans. Alexander Callander Murray, 64-76. Orchard Park, NY: Broadview Press, 2000.

Ptolemy, Claudius. *Geography of Claudius Ptolemy.* Translated and Edited by Edward Luther Stevenson. NY: New York Public Library, 1932; Reprint, New York: Dover Books, 1991. Available at <http://www.ukans.edu/history/index/europe/ancient_ rome/E/Gazetteer/Periods/Roman/Texts/Ptolemy/2/10/home.html>. Page Updated 19 Nov 03. Accessed 3/19/2004.

The Saga of the Volsungs: The Saga of Ragnar Lodbrok together with The Lay of Kraka. Translated by Margaret Schlauch. New York: The AMS Press and W.W. Norton & Company, Inc., 1978, reprint of the 1st edition. Published by American-Scandanavian Foundation, New York, Vol. 35, *Scandinavian Classics*, 1930.

Sidonius, *Epist. 7.II.I.* In Ralph Whitney Mathisen, *Roman Aristocrats in Barbarian Gaul: Strategies for Survival in an Age of Transition*, 29. Austin: University of Texas Press, 1993.

_____. *Poems and Letters.* Vol. 1. Translated with an Introduction by W.B. Anderson. Loeb Classical Series. Cambridge, Mass.: Harvard University Press, 1936.

_____. *Carmina.* ed. and trans. Christian Luetjohann, *MGH Auctores antiquissimi* 8: 173 ff. 1887, in *Sidonius*, ed.

and trans. W.B. Anderson, Loeb Classical Library, 1936. XII: 1-22. In Herwig Wolfram. *The Roman Empire and Its Germanic Peoples*. Translated by Thomas Dunlap. Berkeley, Cal.: University of California Press, 1997., 258-59.

_____. *The Letters of Sidonius*, Translated O.M. Dalton, 2 vols. (Oxford, 1915). In *From Roman to Merovingian Gaul: A Reader,* ed. and trans. Alexander Callander Murray, 193-258. Orchard Park, NY: Broadview Press, 2000.

Socrates. 7.30.3, *Chronica Minora*, ii. In Thompson, E.A. "Christianity and the Northern Barbarians," 72. In *The Conflict Between Paganism and Christianity in the Fourth Century,* ed. Arnaldo Momigliano, 56-78. London: Oxford University Press, 1963, originally published in *Nottingham Medieval Studies*, I, 1957.

_____. vii, 30. In Thompson, E.A. *A History of Attila and the Huns*, 66. London: Oxford University Press, 1948. Reprinted Westport, Conn.: Greenwood Press, 1975.

_____. *The Ecclesiastical History of Socrates Scholasticus*, in *Socrates and Sozomenus: Ecclesiastical Histories.* Revised by A.C. Zenos. Vol. 2, A Select Library of Nicene and Post-Nicene Fathers of the Christian Church: Second Series. Edited and Translated Philip Schaff and Henry Wace. New York: The Christian Literature Company, 1890.

The Song of the Nibelungs: A Verse Translation from the Middle High German Nibelungenlied. Edited by Frank G. Ryder. Detroit: Wayne State University Press, 1962.

Tacitus, *Germania*, in *Tacitus*. Translated by Maurice Hutton and revised by E.H.Warmington. Vol. 1, *Agricola, Germania, Dialogus*. Loeb Classical Series. Cambridge, Mass.: Harvard University Press, 1914. Reprint 1970.

The Writings of Salvian the Presbyter, Translated by Jeremiah F. O'Sullivan. New York, 1947. In *From Roman to Merovingian Gaul: A Reader,* ed. and trans. Alexander Callander Murray, 109-137. Orchard Park, NY: Broadview Press, 2000.

Vita Sanctae Chrotildis, c. XII. In Godefroid Kurth. *Saint Clotilda*. Translated by V.M. Crawford with a preface by G. Tyrell, 105-106. London: Duckworth & Co., 1898.

Vita sancti Lupicini abbatis 10. In Ralph Whitney Mathisen, *Roman Aristocrats in Barbarian Gaul: Strategies for Survival in an Age of Transition*, 101.   Austin: University of Texas Press, 1993.

Vopiscus, Flavius. *Probus*. Translated by David Magie. Vol. 3. *The Scriptores Historiae Augustae*. Loeb Classical Series. Cambridge, Mass.: Harvard University Press, 1932. Reprinted 1934.

Zosimus. *Historia Nova.* Translated by James J. Buchanan and Harold T. Davis. San Antonio, TX: Trinity University Press, 1967.

Secondary Sources - Books

A Companion to the Nibelungenlied. Edited by Winder McConnell. Columbia, SC: Camden House, 1998.

Barnwell, P.S. *Emperor, Prefects, & Kings: The Roman West, 395-565*. Chapel Hill: The University of North Carolina Press, 1992.

Bekker, Hugo. *The Nibelungenlied: a literary analysis*. Toronto: University of Toronto Press, 1971.

Bury, J.B. *The Invasion of Europe by the Barbarians*. New York: W.W. Norton & Company, 1967. Reprint, New York: W.W. Norton & Company, 2000.

_____. *History of the Later Roman Empire: From the Death of Theodosius I. to the Death of Justinian.* 2 vols. London: Macmillan & Co., Ltd., 1923. Reprint New York: Dover Publications, Inc., 1958.

Collins, Roger. *Early Medieval Europe, 300-1000.* 2d ed. New York: Palgrave, 1999.

Dill, Samuel. *Roman Society in Gaul in the Merovingian Age.* London: George Allen & Unwin Ltd., 1926.

Dyson, Stephen L. *The Creation of the Roman Frontier.* Princeton , N.J.: Princeton University Press, 1985.

Early Medieval Kingship. Edited by P.H. Sawyer and I.N. Wood. Leeds, UK: University of Leeds, 1977.

Fifth-century Gaul: a crisis of identity? Edited by John Drinkwater and Hugh Elton. London: Cambridge University Press, 1992.

From Roman to Merovingian Gaul: A Reader. Edited and Translated by Alexander Callander Murray. Orchard Park, NY: Broadview Press, 2000.

Freeman, E.A., *Western Europe in the Fifth Century* (1904). In J.B Bury, *History of the Later Roman Empire: From the Death of Theodosius I. to the Death of Justinian,* 1:189. New York: Dover Publications, Inc., 1958.

Geary, Patrick. *Before France and Germany: The Creation and Transformation of the Merovingian World.* New York: Oxford University Press, 1988.

_____. *The Myth of Nations: The Medieval Origins of Europe.* Princeton: Princeton University Press, 2002.

Gibbon, Edward. *The History of the Decline and Fall of the Roman Empire.* 6 Vols. London, 1776-1788.

_____. *The Decline and Fall of the Roman Empire.* Vol. 40, Great Books of the Western World. Chicago: Encyclopedia Britannica, 1952.

Goffart, Walter. *Barbarians and Romans, A.D. 418-584: The*

Techniques of Accommodation. Princeton: Princeton University Press, 1980.

Heinzelmann, Martin. *Bischofsherrschaft in Gallien: Zur Kontinuitat romischer Fuhrungsschichten von 4. Bis zum 7. Jahrhundert*. Munich, 1976. In Ralph Whitney Mathisen. *Ecclesiastical Factionalism and Religious Controversy in Fifth-Century Gaul*, 153-57. Washington, D.C.: The Catholic University Press, 1989.

Hen, Yitzhak. *Culture and Religion in Merovingian Gaul A.D. 481-751*. Leiden, The Netherlands: E.J. Brill, 1995.

Hollister, C. Warren. *Medieval Europe: A Short History*, 8th ed. New York: McGraw-Hill, 1998.

James, Edward. *The Origins of France: From Clovis to the Capetians, 500-1000*. New York: St. Martin's Press, 1982.

_____. *The Franks*. Oxford, UK: Basil Blackwell Ltd., 1988.

King, Anthony. *Roman Gaul and Germany*. Berkeley: University of California Press, 1990.

Kurth, Godefroid. *Saint Clotilda*. Translated by V.M. Crawford with a preface by G. Tyrell. London: Duckworth & Co., 1898.

Lacroix, Paul. *Science and Literature in the Middle Ages and the Renaissance*. New York: Frederick Unger Publishing Co., 1878.

Langgartner, Georg. *Die Galliepolitik der Papste im 5. Und 6. Jahrhundert. Eine Studie uber den apostolische Vikariat von Arles*. Bonn, 1964. In Ralph Whitney Mathisen. *Ecclesiastical Factionalism and Religious Controversy in Fifth-Century Gaul*, 153-57. Washington, D.C.: The Catholic University Press, 1989.

Latouche, Robert. *Caesar to Charlemagne: The Beginnings of France*. Translated by Jennifer Nicholson. London: Phoenix House, 1968.

Jones, A.H.M. *The later Roman Empire, 284-602: a social, economic and administrative survey*. 3 Vols. Oxford, 1964. In P.S. Barnwell. *Emperor, Prefects, & Kings: The Roman West, 395-565*, 82. Chapel Hill: The University of North Carolina Press, 1992.

Leblant, E. *Inscriptions Chretiennes de la Gaule* (Paris, 1865). In Godefroid Kurth. *Saint Clotilda*. Translated by V.M. Crawford with a Preface by G. Tyrell, 20. London: Duckworth & Co., 1898.

Maenchen-Helfen, Otto. *The World of the Huns*. Berkeley and Los Angeles: University of California Press, 1973. In Herwig Wolfram. *The Roman Empire and Its Germanic Peoples*, 258. Translated by Thomas Dunlap. Berkeley, Cal.: University of California Press, 1997.

Mathisen, Ralph Whitney. *Ecclesiastical Factionalism and Religious Controversy in Fifth-Century Gaul*. Washington, D.C.: The Catholic University Press, 1989.

_____. *Roman Aristocrats in Barbarian Gaul: Strategies for Survival in an Age of Transition*. Austin: University of Texas Press, 1993.

Musset, Lucien. *The Germanic Invasions: The Making of Europe AD 400-600*. Translated by Edward and Columba James. University Park, Penn.: The Pennsylvania State University Press, 1975.

O'Sullivan, Jeremiah and John F. Burns. *Medieval Europe*. New York: F.S. Crofts & Co., 1943.

Randers-Pehrson, Justine Davis. *Barbarians and Romans: The Birth Struggle of Europe, A.D. 400-700*. Norman: University of Oklahoma Press, 1983.

Riche, Pierre. *Education and Culture in the Barbarian West: From the Sixth Through the Eighth Century*. Translated by John J. Contreni, With a foreword by Richard E. Sullivan. Columbia: University of South Carolina Press,

1976. In Russell, James C. *The Germanization of Early Medieval Christianity: A Sociohistorical Approach to Religious Transformation*, 143-44. New York: Oxford University Press, 1994.

Russell, James C. *The Germanization of Early Medieval Christianity: A Sociohistorical Approach to Religious Transformation*. New York: Oxford University Press, 1994.

Rydberg, Viktor. *Teutonic Mythology: Gods And Goddesses Of The Northland*. Translated by Rasmus B. Anderson, Memorial Edition, 3 Vols., *Norrœna Anglo-Saxon classics,* Vol. 1. London: Norrœna Society, 1907.

_____. *Teutonic Mythology: Gods And Goddesses Of The Northland*. Translated by Rasmus B. Anderson, Memorial Edition, 3 Vols., *Norrœna Anglo-Saxon classics,* Vol. 3. London: Norrœna Society, 1907.

Sainted Women of the Dark Ages. Edited and Translated by JoAnn McNamara and John E. Halborg with E. Gordon Whatley. Durham, N.C.: Duke University Press, 1992.

Scherman, Katharine. *The Birth of France: Warriors, Bishops and Long-Haired Kings*. New York: Random House, 1987.

Schmidt, L. *Geschichte der Wandalen*, 1901. In J.B Bury, *History of the Later Roman Empire: From the Death of Theodosius I. to the Death of Justinian,* 1:187. New York: Dover Publications, Inc., 1958.

Schulenburg, Jane Tibbetts. *Forgetful of Their Sex: Female Sanctity and Society ca. 500-1100*. Chicago: University of Chicago Press, 1998.

The Barbarian Invasions: Catalyst of a New Order. Edited by Katherine Fischer Drew. New York: Holt, Rinehart and Winston, 1970.

The Conflict Between Paganism and Christianity in the Fourth

Century. Edited by Arnaldo Momigliano. London: Oxford University Press, 1963.

Thompson, E.A. *A History of Attila and the Huns.* London: Oxford University Press, 1948. Reprinted Westport, Conn.: Greenwood Press, 1975.

————. *The Visigoths in the Time of Ulfila.* Oxford: Clarendon Press, 1966. In James C. Russell. *The Germanization of Early Medieval Christianity: A Sociohistorical Approach to Religious Transformation,* 139-40. New York: Oxford University Press, 1994.

Todd, Malcolm. *Everyday Life of The Barbarians: Goths, Franks, and Vandals.* New York: Dorset Press, 1972.

————. *The Northern Barbarians: 100 B.C.-A.D. 300.* London: Hutchinson University Library, 1975.

Tolkien, J.R.R. and Christopher, *The Legend of Sigurd and Gudrún.* New York: Harper Collins, 2009.

Wallace-Hadrill, J.M. *The Long-Haired Kings and other Studies in Frankish History.* New York: Barnes & Noble, Inc., 1962.

————. *The Barbarian West, 400-1000.* Oxford: Blackwell Publishers Inc., 1999.

Wemple, Suzanne Fonay. *Women in Frankish Society: Marriage and the Cloister 500 to 900.* Philadelphia: University of Pennsylvania Press, 1981.

Wickham, Chris. *Early Medieval Italy: Central Power and Local Society 400-1000,* Totowa, NJ, 1981. In Patrick Geary. *The Myth of Nations: The Medieval Origins of Europe,* 39. Princeton: Princeton University Press, 2002.

Whittaker, C.R. *Frontiers of the Roman Empire: A Social and Economic Study.* Baltimore: The Johns Hopkins University Press, 1994.

Wolfram, Herwig. *The Roman Empire and Its Germanic Peoples.* Translated by Thomas Dunlap. Berkeley, Cal.:

University of California Press, 1997.

Wood, Ian. *The Merovingian Kingdoms, 450-751*. London: Longman Group, 1995.

Secondary Sources – Articles and Essays

Baynes, Norman H. "A Note on Professor Bury's 'History of the Later Roman Empire'." *The Journal of Roman Studies* 12 (1922): 207-29.

Burns, C. Delisle. "Christianity and the First Europe." In *The Barbarian Invasions: Catalyst of a New Order,* ed. Katherine Fischer Drew, 84-91. New York: Holt, Rinehart and Winston, 1970.

Dill, Samuel. "Persistence of the Aristocratic Way of Life." In *The Barbarian Invasions: Catalyst of a New Order*, ed. Katherine Fischer Drew, 15-26. New York: Holt, Rinehart and Winston, 1970.

Dumville, David N. "Kingship, Genealogies and Regnal Lists." In *Early Medieval Kingship*. Edited by P.H. Sawyer and I.N. Wood, 72-104. Leeds, UK: University of Leeds, 1977.

Elton , Hugh. "Defence in fifth century Gaul." In *Fifth-century Gaul: a crisis of identity?* ed. John Drinkwater and Hugh Elton, 167-76. Cambridge: Cambridge University Press, 1992.

Goffart, Walter."Rome, Constantinople, and the Barbarians." *The American Historical Review* 86, no.2 (1981): 275-306.

Gordon, C.D. "Subsidies in Roman Imperial Defence." *Phoenix* 3, no.2 (1949): 60-9.

Halphen, Louis. "Germanic Society in the Early Sixth Century." In *The Barbarian Invasions: Catalyst of a New Order*, ed. by Katherine Fischer Drew, 27-41. New York: Holt,

Rinehart and Winston: 1970.

Heather, Peter. "The Huns and the End of the Roman Empire in Western Europe." *The English Historical Review* 110, no.435 (1995): 4-41.

Hemple, George. "The Linguistic and Ethnografic Status of the Burgundians." *Transactions and Proceedings of the American Philological Association* 39, (1908): 105-119.

James, Edward. "The Merovingian archaeology of south-west Gaul." *British Archaeological Reports*, Supplemental Series 25, (Oxford, 1977). In C.R. Whittaker. *Frontiers of the Roman Empire: A Social and Economic Study*, 233. Baltimore: The Johns Hopkins University Press, 1994.

Kuhn, Herbert. "Asiatic Influences on the Art of the Migrations." *Parnassus* 9, no.1 (1937): 13-16, 43.

Latouche, Robert. "Agriculture in the Early Middle Ages." In *The Barbarian Invasions: Catalyst of a New Order*, ed. Katherine Fischer Drew, 84-91. New York: Holt, Rinehart and Winston, 1970.

Malone, Kemp. "Ptolemy's Skandia." *The American Journal of Philology* 45, no.4 (1924): 362-70.

Mathisen, Ralph Whitney. "Barbarian Bishops and the Churches 'in Barbaricis Gentibus' During Late Antiquity." *Speculum* 72, no.3 (1997): 664-697.

Mirkovic, Miroslava. "The Later Roman Colonate and Freedom." *Transactions of the American Philosophical Society* 87, no.2 (1997): i-viii, and 1-144.

Murdoch, Brian. "Politics in the Niebelungenlied." In *A Companion to the Nibelungenlied*. Edited by Winder McConnell, 229-50. Columbia, SC: Camden House, 1998.

Nelson, Janet. "Queens as Jezebels: The careers of Brunhild and Balthild in Merovingian History." In *Medieval*

Women. Dedicated and presented to Professor Rosalind M.T. Hill on the occasion of her seventieth birthday, ed. D. Baker, 31-77. Oxford, 1978. In Elisabeth van Houts, "The State of Research: Women in Medieval History and Literature." *Journal of Medieval History* 20 (1994): 287.

Schonberger, H. "The Roman Frontier in Germany: An Archaeological Survey." *The Journal of Roman Studies* 59, no. ½ (1969): 144-97.

Thompson, E.A. "The Settlement of the Barbarians in Southern Gaul." *The Journal of Roman Studies* .46, parts 1 and 2 (1956): 65-75.

_____. "Christianity and the Northern Barbarians." In *The Conflict Between Paganism and Christianity in the Fourth Century,* ed. Arnaldo Momigliano, 56-78. London: Oxford University Press, 1963, originally published in *Nottingham Medieval Studies,* I, 1957.

_____. "The Germans in the Time of Caesar." In *The Barbarian Invasions: Catalyst of a New Order,* ed. Katherine Fischer Drew, 70-6. New York: Holt, Rinehart and Winston, 1970.

van Houts, Elisabeth. "The State of Research: Women in Medieval History and Literature." *Journal of Medieval History* 20 (1994): 277-292.

Wood, Ian N. "Kings, Kingdoms and Consent." In *Early Medieval Kingship.* Edited by P.H. Sawyer and I.N. Wood, 6-29. Leeds, U.K.:University of Leeds, 1977.

_____. "Continuity or Calamity?: the Constraints of Literary Models." In *Fifth-century Gaul: a crisis of identity?* Edited by John Drinkwater and Hugh Elton, 9-18. Cambridge: Cambridge University Press, 1992.

_____. "Incest, Law and the Bible in Sixth-century Gaul." *Early Medieval Europe* 7, no.3 (1998): 291-304.

_____. "*Gentes*, Kings and Kingdoms—The Emergence of Sates: The Kingdom of the Gibichungs." In *Regna and gentes : the relationship between late antique and early medieval peoples and kingdoms in the transformation of the Roman worl*. Edited by Hans-Werner Goetz, Jörg Jarnut and Walter Pohl, 243-269. Boston: Brill, 2003.

Wunderlich, Werner. "The Authorship of the Nibelungenlied." In *A Companion to the Nibelungenlied*. Edited by Winder McConnell, 251-77. Columbia, SC: Camden House, 1998.

INDEX

D

E

F

G

H

I

J

ABOUT THE AUTHOR

Marc Comtois has a B.S. in Marine Engineering from the United States Merchant Marine Academy and an M.A. in History from Providence College. He is a native New Englander who resides in Rhode Island with his wife and two daughters.

Made in the USA
Lexington, KY
26 March 2012